Huddersfield VOICES

Errol Hannon

TEMPUS

I would like to thank all of the following for the use of their photographs, illustrations and documents:

George Slater, Mike Hirst, Vera Waddington, Arthur Quarmby, Liz Colquhoun, Ray Wilson, David Gronow and the Huddersfield Rugby League Players Association, Alan Chapman, Stuart Coldwell, John Mitchell, David Green, Alex Plytnik, Janina Stanowska, Geoff Hill, and also Peter Bray of Honley, *Huddersfield Examiner* and the Kirklees Image Archive in the Tolson Museum.

First published 2007

Tempus Publishing Limited
The Mill, Brimscombe Port,
Stroud, Gloucestershire, GL5 2QG

British Library Cataloguing in Publication Data.
A catalogue record for this book is available from the British Library.

ISBN 978 0 7524 3714 9

Typesetting and origination by Tempus Publishing Limited
Printed in Great Britain

Huddersfield

VOICES

Contents

We's wi frum?

Voices of the Past

The origins of Yorkshire folk, particularly the industrialized West Riding variety, who tend to have more callouses and gritty edges on the collective imagination than the green welly folk in the old North Riding, or the windswept North Sea crowd from the flatter lands of the East Riding, are oft the focus of considerable debate, some of it anguished. The local philosophy – Yokksha through n' through, to the bone, 'offcumduns/comersin' viewed with suspicion – can find itself out of kilter with tradition if undesirables from the past start elbowing their way to the front. Go back a sufficient distance and we find that Marsden was populated by orphaned street urchins from London brought in as really cheap labour. No doubt 'dahn sarf' was glad to be rid. That might account for it, Marsden that is, a Huddersfield 'suburb' with its own idiosyncratic brand of celebration, etc.

Considering both the effect of and on more recent incomers, some time ago I was in a pub hard by the town centre. Four old chaps were sitting around a table drinking their pints, smoking their fags, playing cards

The Colne Calley from Heights.

and giving absolutely no offence to anyone. I was standing close by and observing. One was very obviously a Sikh, the chap next to him an easy-going Muslim: there was an elderly Irishman and an old and distinguished-looking West Indian gentleman. If only the rest of us would so readily accommodate each other. It was the Sikh fellow's turn to buy a round so I engaged him in a little light conversation while he was at the bar. Never mind his thoughts about the UK, how did he feel about 'uddersfield? Did it feel like home? After all, it's not exactly the Punjab. He looked at me a little sagely. 'So, where the bloody 'ell's tha bin, ahr kid? Dun't tha knaw Yokksha's God's Own?' And there we have it. Was it something about Huddersfield or simply the perversity of folk everywhere that enabled this delightful cameo?

Never mind the great melting pot on the other side of the pond, Huddersfield has stewed away nicely since way back into the first millennium and, initially, it was all to do with topography. To the east lie the lowlands of the vast Vale of York and Wakefield, the capital of the West Riding by virtue of its Episcopal rank. The approaches to Huddersfield from the west and south are routed through three great dales, the river valleys of the Holme, Colne and Calder, gouged out of the harsh gritstone/sandstone moorland of the high Pennines, the backbone of northern England. The soil is dark and produces a particularly depressing aspect in wet weather, wholly unlike the aesthetically pleasing light-green carpet on the limestone of the adjacent North Riding and South Derbyshire Dales.

The Holme Valley, with its capital, Holmfirth, is smaller, more attractive and was never as industrialized as the others. Put firmly on the map by 'Last o' t' summer wine', a seemingly endless dirge that's been on the box for so long that few can actually remember what Holmfirth was like before it (i.e. nobody outside the area had ever heard of it). How many can remember Blamire? It was, of course, the one-time home of Bamforth's saucy postcards with fat ladies, henpecked hubbies and well-upholstered lasses – all long gone, along with Blamire.

The Colne, stripped out, butchered and plastered with mills by two centuries of Gradgrinds, is long and raw and perhaps symbolically is the heartland of a wide constituency with a politically Liberal tradition, courtesy of the twentieth century and an undeniably bitter Luddite past. Since Richard Wainwright's memorable tenure the Libs have been a little restricted to the back seat, no doubt an aberration that will be addressed. The valley's timber is now only a memory though Tree Society worthies struggle to restore it; westerlies roar in from Manchester to rip through it from Marches dun, or dene (Marsden, the march hill, the edge/end of the valley). Denied windbreaks, layers of substantial underwear were famously required by its inhabitants prior to what may or might just pretend to be global warming. Its capital is probably Marsden, although Slaithwaite, in the centre of the valley, would no doubt fight for the privilege. A curious place, with its two pronunciations: 'Slathwaite', possibly far closer to the Old Norse original than the slackjawed 'Sla'wit'. Recently, it's become Skelthwaite, focal point of yet another telly-epic starring loads of folk who are about as West Riding as Billy Connolly.

The Calder is the largest of the dales, reaching up to 'Tod' (Todmorden), whose natives roll their Rs and sound more than suspiciously Lancastrian. A little further on is the engagingly named Portsmouth.

The highest point of the Almannesbyrig.

The ridge from Castle Hill to Almondbury.

Upper Calderdale largely lies outside the geographical limits of this work as it comes within the purview of Halifax. A different town, outside t' solar system according to some Huddersfield folk yet Halifax kept its lovely old market hall while Huddersfield 'got shut' in favour of a hideous piazza and horrid bungalow. The attempt to join the two towns at the hip via the Calderdale & Kirklees NHS Trust, while the two authorities remain politically separate, has apparently been very expensive and bitterly resented.

The three rivers forming the landscape have Celtic names, as do most of the nation's natural waterways. The incoming Angles, fleeing their waterlogged homeland of Angeln in Denmark (*c.* fifth or sixth century), perhaps regarded the indigenous Cymric (Welsh-speaking) Celtic Britons as twilight people, folk associated with the dark side. The Celtic hero was of course Arthur, who, in his battles against the English invaders, had wizards and swords rising out of magical ponds. The Angles (English) were more pragmatic, getting their hands dirty with hard work.

Viking arrivals in around the ninth century came from the east and west. The similarity between the Danes and the north-eastern English, from The Wash to Bamburgh, is glaringly obvious and given the overlapping history it would hardly have been otherwise. With that in mind, we know that the Old Norse and Danes would nest in Calderdale, to give it its Celt/Viking name, the Calder Valley, if you prefer the all-Celtic flavour, or Calderdale Valley, if you're into tautology and are not sure which is preferable. A few miles down the Calder to the east lies the mini-city of Wakefield, which had a handful of Norse resident in Normanton.

Huddersfield's Old Market Hall. (Kirklees Archive)

Nowt to do with Normans, you understand, or indeed anyone called Norman, but Wakefield was nonetheless an Anglo-Danish town with the multiplicity of thorpe (dorp) place names – Alverthorpe, Wrenthorpe, Kettlethorpe – surrounding its English heart a dead giveaway. This may well account for the difference in accent and almost certainly old dialect between the two towns. Did Wakefield's surplus Danes move westwards up the Calder to encroach upon the environs of Huddersfield with its strong Norse flavour? They certainly put down roots hard by, in Denby Dale (Dan by daela – the Danish settlement in the valley), within modern Huddersfield's political limits, and they may well have camped in the town itself.

There's an amusing and interesting story about a West Riding teenager being interviewed by a local police officer; she had witnessed an incident involving a group of youngsters. Asked what these kids were up to she replied, 'Thay wain deein oawt, juz lekkin'. Two visiting officers, one from the Met and the other from Denmark, were listening in. The lad from London was utterly mystified by this impenetrable gobbledegook, but the Copenhagen chap knew exactly what she was talking about, understanding every syllable of the youngster's very, very old Danish.

Huddersfield's Norse community apparently hauled themselves up the Almannesbyrig, the rock fortress for/of all men, now Almondbury Hill, stretching from the village of Almondbury to the summit of 'Casselill', as it is in the local patois. Why that particular Norse name, we don't know: the etymology is difficult and the original intent of the name possibly lost. Perhaps it was an exercise in local government: go up and listen to the big cheese. Similar setups prevail to this day in Iceland and the ex-Norse Isle of Man. Did the Norse grow *bygg* (barley) in Big Valley or did the Angles see it as the *byge* (bending) valley? The Norse apparently cultivated flax (*lin*) and sloes (*slah*) in clearings (*thveitr*) at Linthwaite and Slaithwaite in the Colne Valley. Conversation with these newcomers might have been a little jaw wrenching for the by-now indigenous northern English. However, as their forebears had hailed from Denmark and Friesland it would have been fairly readily achieved. Tough times no doubt encouraged rapid melding.

The Irish have long been in western England, longer in fact than the English. A 'rights of residence' dispute could be illuminating. They certainly came in as another wave with the Norse as the Norse-Danish/Irish kingdom of Dublin and York spread across Cumbria, Lancashire and Yorkshire in the ninth century.

The English/Scandinavian/Irish/local Celtic town had expanded far beyond the limits of the original patch cleared from the forest and at some time called Oderesfeld. How soon was the name adopted? Was the character who ran this tiny settlement an Angle whose name eludes us beyond Oder or was he Nordic Ottar? Again, we don't know. The stew would bubble away until the Channel Islands-speaking Normans muscled in as conquerors and followed the Norse up the hill with more serious intent, leaving earthwork remains of what might have been a dominating motte and bailey structure.

This tribal mush would keep its flavour until the mid-nineteenth century when a sea of poverty- and famine-stricken Irish arrived in the north of England and south-western Scotland. These despairing folk were the first of the 'modern' migrants in that they arrived in such huge numbers as to generate contempt and unveiled hostility.

In time this would be overcome, as it always is, and many dyed-in-the-wool townspeople with obviously Gaelic or corrupted Irish names, and we're talking considerable numbers, will have no knowledge of the provenance of, or recollection of, the arrival of their forefathers.

Popular subscription, forked out willingly or otherwise, one suspects, sufficed to plant the monument to Queen Victoria's jubilee on top of Castle Hill. It was, of course, as much a celebration of success in the woollen industry as it was of Victoria's fiftieth year in the chair. The same woollen industry was now firmly established as the engine of the town's economy and in its heyday, so goes the tale, Huddersfield would boast more Rolls Royce cars per head of population than anywhere else. How well this was received on the factory floor is another matter. Success was measurable and the extremely successful Ramsden family would, for a nice wedge, part with the town centre they actually owned to the corporation. The voices of all of these long-gone folk have survived in the speech patterns, folklore and the grim humour that typifies the area.

New accents were added after 1945. Ex-service Poles and western Ukrainians added their own distinct flavour, quite literally so as between them they make some of the most delectable bread in the West Riding. A trawl through local directories reveals owski, icki, czyk, wak, iek, etc name suffixes in some profusion. From the 1950s onwards,

Market Hall interior. (Kirklees Archive)

Harold Wilson bustles before Pevsner's favourite rail façade.

folk seeking something better arrived from the ex-Imperial subcontinent, as well as East and West Africa and the West Indies. As with their predecessors, they would add their cultures and all have melded without too many bumps and bruises.

Many had come to work in what had once been a prosperous woollen industry. Its post-Second World War decline has been famously attributed to a variety of causal factors: Labour governments; trade union casuistry; greed; failure to invest appropriately; lack of forward planning; out-of-the-ark working practices; lack of any planning; taxation; export strangulation/regulation; more greed; Conservative governments; winning the war; Europe, in any shape or form; failing to lose the war; demise of the empire, *et al.* Unsurprisingly, those favoured explanations have unerringly depended upon the social, political and economic standing of the advocate. Belt tightening and reasonable business acumen have conspired to hopefully ensure the survival of the remnant. Time will inevitably tell. The vast and imposing mill buildings of many of those that have gone to the wall now survive as conversions into apartments.

Huddersfield then is as it was, third in line behind Leeds and Bradford in the seniority of the West Riding, not as elegant as the former and nowhere near as ugly as the latter. The West Riding as a political and social entity has gone, along with its northern neighbour. Yet, some of us older types continue to use the original rather than that political contraption, West Yorkshire, fortunately gone to the shades. The Angle/Danish inhabitants of Yorkshire and Lincolnshire divided their scires/shires into 'thridings' or thirds, which usefully serves to answer the oft-bleated question, 'Why dunt/dint Yokksha 'ave a South Riding?' Of the six the East Riding of Yorkshire survives and that only by dint of restoration. Huddersfield now lords it over the southern half of the Metropolitan County of Kirklees and of that opinions do seriously vary. The name was bushwhacked by local government from ancient Kirklees Priory, which lies twixt the M62 and The Three Nuns, a well-known hostelry on the north side of town. Rumour has it that the priory provided the deathbed for one R. Hood, outlaw. The fall of an arrow shot from his window would mark his resting-place. Mmm!

The voices who have been sufficiently kind or impolitic to contribute to this book represent the hopes, the interests, the endeavours, the pastimes, the social habits and, to some extent, the mores of this area. Some of them have never lived anywhere else, others were from elsewhere but are now here, some no longer live here yet retain fond and often mischievous memories of the town that bore them. My sincerest thanks go out to them for their patience and effort. Their contributions are either in the form of taped interviews or extracts from more informal conversations and used with their agreement. We tend not to write as we speak, a habit long since coached out of us in the necessary quest for standardized English. However, in these extracts I have tried to record what people have said, how they said it and, to some extent, how they speak.

Ray Wilson

Huddersfield and Everton, 1966 England World Cup-winning player

I'm originally from the Derbyshire mining village of Shirebrook and I played for the local open-age side on Saturday mornings. I remember they had to rake me out of bed first morning as I'd been working all night. We lost 6-3 and I scored the hat trick for our side. From there I had a trial for Ray Goodall and everything's gone fine since then. A scout was there from Everton and he offered a shirt but I were a bit innocent at that age and said, 'No, Huddersfield have given me the chance'. That was '51/52ish, I was sixteen, a full-time professional at seventeen and then did my National Service with the Royal Artillery in Egypt. I don't know if you can remember but clubs had to give you six months when you came out of the Army to gather yourself together again.

When I compare soccer now with what it was then, well, it was a working-class game. Soccer playing wasn't a 'proper job', not like a joiner, say, who could have his military service deferred until twenty-one. Between eighteen and twenty is the most important time in your life and two years is a long time in soccer. Everybody had changed when I came back 'cos I went there as inside left, then outside left, then went to left half, then left-back. I wrote to my brother, if they move me again I'll be bloody left out. I wasn't too happy as I'd been a pretty serious inside forward as a Derby schoolboy.

Ray as a teenager. (R. Wilson)

I was twenty-nine when I moved to Everton in 1964 after 300,000 clubs had tried to sign me from the First Division. I

Airbourne at Leeds Road. (R. Wilson)

was unhappy about leaving, in a sense. I'd married a Huddersfield girl and loved the area. I'd thirty international caps and never played in the First Division except a couple of times before Town were relegated. Then I got into the England side and I thought I ought to be allowed to move on and play at that level regularly, and Huddersfield at that time were never going to get there. They wouldn't go into the market. I can't remember anyone on the books they'd paid more than £500 for. We were always middle of the table, occasionally a bit higher in the Second Division.

I'd get on my 'ands and knees for a move as it's only a short career, ten maybe fifteen years, you're going downhill when you're thirty. The lads I was playing with in the England team were talking to their clubs about me. Busby tried to sign me at Manchester United but Town wouldn't let me go. I never said I wouldn't play or try hard for them as I was a good pro. Shankly wanted me to sign for Liverpool, every club was approaching me but they didn't have to let you go.

I was married with two kids and lived in one of Town's own houses so to be honest they had you by the short and curlies. Once you'd signed as a kid, you'd signed for life, not for one season. If they wanted you until you were fifty they could, we threatened to go on strike and then it all changed. It wasn't about wanting to leave the Town, but if I'd never been able to leave can you imagine how disappointed I'd have been?

As soon as I went to Everton, no disrespect to Huddersfield, but there were seventeen international players couldn't get into the bloody team at Everton, a massive side with 60/70,000 every home game. When I started training I thought crikey, this is where you should have been all the time.

When I started for Town I used to live at Oakes in their property as no player could afford his own house in those days. I was only on £40 a week when I was at Everton. You might be a working-class hero – you were certainly getting working-class money. After my mum died, back in Shirebrook, I worked on the railway and I could earn in a good week £11/12, at seventeen. Then I signed for Huddersfield for £5, that's a great career move! I've been going downhill ever since. I'd some problems as there were six of us in digs together, in one bedroom. We had to pay for our digs, £2 10s a week and we had to pay our bus fares to get to the ground. The only entertainment we had was going to the cinema and there were plenty of them in Huddersfield. You could get in for tuppence or threepence. Seating was rough and there was no guarantee you wouldn't get a spring up your arse.

Dennis Law was there, Gordon Lowe and his mate, a lad called Jack Connor. I would be his best man. There were two other lads, as I said, six of us in the room. I do think there should have been a bit more money knocking about. I mean, when I was at Town the gates were great, 30/40,000 or you'd be disappointed.

You're a West Ham supporter and when I were at Everton I can never remember playing a game against West Ham and getting beat. We actually went there when Huddersfield were a Second Division side and beat the buggers 5–1. Whatya think of that then!

Young Wilson in Town colours. (R. Wilson)

You know, after football where do you go? I was fortunate as my father-in-law was a funeral director and he started me from scratch to learn the job. I wanted to have a real go at it, embalming exams, etc. I went to Nottingham to take me test, I was in me forties then and I sat in this room with all these bloody kids and I thought what am I doing here? Anyway, I managed to sneak through, had no O levels in those days.

The January 1957 game at Charlton, the epic, 7-6 game. Aye, I remember all of it, hah, hah! We'd been 5-1 in front and we'd never beaten them, they were definitely our bogey team, so we thought we had it wrapped up. They were down to ten men and they were losing 5-1 with twenty minutes to go so they threw everything forward. We were a bit casual. The thing that makes me laugh, the thing I really remember was

THIRD EDN.

FOR ALL YOUR
OFFICE FURNITURE
MACHINES, ETC.
CONSULT
BUSINESS EQUIPMENT CO., LTD.
8, STANDARD HOUSE Tel. Hudd. 4433

Huddersfield Daily Examiner

29,823 (Registered for transmission in the United Kingdom.) SATURDAY, DECEMBER 21, 1957 PRICE 2½d.

Three Nuns Inn, Mirfield
Telephone: Mirfield 3219 or 2034
A favourite choice of discerning diners who demand cuisine of high order
New kitchens Expert chefs
luncheons and dinners
JOHN MURRY

STARVED OF POSSESION —BUT FARTOWNERS WIN

Wakefield's Uphill Fight

ST. HELENS, entertaining Wakefield Trinity, went ahead with an early try by the South African Van Vollenhoven.

Rhodes failed to kick the goal, but he was later successful from a SILCOCK try.

Hunslet's Revival Receives A Jolt

THE return of Kilroy and the injury to Cecil were the cause of changes in the Huddersfield back division for the game with Hunslet this afternoon.

These re-arrangements resulted in Plunkett going on the wing, Colburn going to the centre and Ramsden to stand-off. Hunslet, who came to Huddersfield in the hope of continuing their recent revival, were at full strength except that Boland came in for Platt (K) in the second row.

... later recovered it from a dropped Hunslet pass.

Thornley and Fairbank were ...

Results At A Glance

LEAGUE—DIVISION I

3—0	Arsenal	3	Sunderland	0
0—0	Aston V	0	Birmingh'm	2
1—1	Bolton	1	Luton	2
0—0	Burnley	3	Portsm'th	1
0—2	Chelsea	2	Tottenham	4
1—0	Leeds	2	Blackpool	1
1—0	Man U	4	Leicester	0
0—0	Newcastle	3	West Brom	0
1—0	Preston	2	Notts F	0
2—3	Sheff W	4	Man C	5
1—0	Wolves	2	Everton	0

	P	W	D	L	Pts
Wolves (6)	23	16	5	2	37
West Brom A (11)	23	9	11	3	29
Manchester C (16)	22	13	1	8	27
Preston NE (3)	22	12	3	7	27
Manchester U (1)	22	12	3	7	27
Luton T (16)	22	12	2	8	26
Arsenal (5)	23	11	3	9	25
Bolton W (9)	22	10	4	8	24
Tottenham H (12)	23	10	4	9	24
Notts F ([illegible])	22	11	2	9	24
Burnley (7)	22	10	3	9	23
Everton (15)	22	7	8	7	22
Blackpool (4)	22	9	4	9	22
Chelsea (13)	22	8	6	8	22
Birmingham C (12)	23	7	7	9	21
Portsmouth (19)	22	7	4	11	18

SCOTTISH LEAGUE—DIV I

0—1	Airdrie	2	Raith	1
0—2	Celtic	2	Partick	3
0—1	Dundee	2	Falkirk	4
1—0	East Fife	2	Motherwell	1
3—1	Hearts	5	St Mirren	1
0—3	Kilmarnock	1	Hibernian	4
0—1	Queen of S	1	Aberdeen	2
1—0	Queens P	1	Clyde	4
3—0	Rangers	5	T Lanark	1

SCOTTISH LEAGUE—DIV II

4—1	Cowdenb'th	6	Ayr	5
0—0	E Stirling	0	Alloa	2
0—1	Forfar	0	Albion	1
2—0	Hamilton	2	Arbroath	2
1—1	Montrose	3	Dundee U	2
5—0	Morton	8	Berwick	0
2—0	St Johnstone	3	Brechin	3
4—0	Stirling A	4	Dumbarton	1
0—2	Stranraer	0	Dunf'rml'ne	3

SUMMERS GETS FIVE IN FANTASTIC GAME

Town, In Front 5—1, Beaten 7—6!

DENIS LAW wore an Arsenal jersey today. Town's seventeen-year-old inside-right went to Highbury this morning for a fitness test, and as a result had to withdraw from the team to meet Charlton at The Valley this afternoon.

In view of the Christmas programme, Mr. Bill Shankly, the Town manager, decided not to risk playing Law, who had thigh and ankle injuries. Howard deputised at inside-right, but there ...

Bury Fight Injury Handicap

THOUGH their outside-right, Robinson, was carried off the field at Park Avenue after five minutes after being hurt in a tackle, Bury overcame the handicap to lead 3—0 at half-time.

Despite the handicap of a four-man attack Bury were distinctly the superior side.

WATSON scored after nine minutes, and in the last five ...

Examiner reports 'that' game, December 1957. (*Huddersfield Examiner*)

the *Daily Express* reporter writing that the reason we were beaten was because of Ray Wilson's inability to stop Charlton's left-winger, Summers. Would have been bloody clever as I were playing left-back, I'd have had to do some sprinting. We drew 'em in't cup at home and terrace were crowded with about 50,000 expecting a similar score. Yep, 0-0!

Shanks (Bill Shankly) was the manager then. Result kept 'im quiet on the way home. Town, oh, they made an absolute b******s of it when they let Shanks go. All the time we were a Second Division side while he was there and even before that, every time we played Liverpool we never lost. Always the same, we either drew or beat them. When he was manager we stuffed 'em by five. He came into the dressing room and said, 'What the bloody hell am I going there for?' Yep, inside six months or so he'd got promotion for them.

Shanks was going to be well suited at Liverpool, with his almost childlike enthusiasm for the game. When he came to the Town he changed everything. All we used to do for training was run round the pitch for three hours, bloody barmy, he changed it all. He was coaching the reserves and got 'em going with five-a-side and sprinting. Then the first team went to him, they wanted him as coach and he got them enjoying themselves training. He was a massive competitor. He would come into the dressing room, 'You, back here at two o clock, and you, you too. Make sure you're here.' We wondered what we'd doing wrong, what the 'eck's going on. He'd come out round the back of the car park. 'Eeh aaah, rrright, England versus Scotland, aaah'. I looked around, there were four Scots and five Englishmen. We got us 'eads together about half past three – let him score the winning goal and we can all bugger off.

I used to go to the cinema at Salendine Nook and 'e were always in there, especially if a Jimmy Cagney gangster were on. He used to sit a couple of rows back going, 'Uuh, ah, ooh, ooh, you ooh you durty rats'. Chin out and all the Cagney hand gestures, the fingers going forward, 'You durty rats'. I don't think we had a manager worth it at Huddersfield after him. He wanted to sign Ian St John and two others from Scotland for next to nothing. Town wouldn't have it so Shankly left and signed them up for

Ray, 2006.

Liverpool – all internationals. I think a lot of Huddersfield people enjoyed a good moan most of all. Maybe things are changing, I'm a bit happier about Town now but I can't see them back in the top flight. Look at Bolton and Blackburn, in a sense bigger football teams than us in towns much the same size. We seem to hang on, skin of the teeth but you never know.

During my thirteen years at the Town I never went in and said I've had enough. I always had some loyalty to the club but I felt things were going to the wall and they did. Without doubt the biggest mistake of all, the biggest the club ever made, was letting Shankly go. I did over ten years service with the club but they wouldn't give me a benefit, even though that was standard. Laugh, there's guys there now on several grand a week and then they're getting a benefit. Ah dear! A benefit in those days was just renting the ground. You set up two or three people to organize it for you. They got a few international players and paid rent to the club. Anyway, it didn't happen.

I moved back to Huddersfield a year before I finished at Everton. I was thirty-four then and I'd thoroughly enjoyed it. It would have been a personal tragedy if I hadn't gone there. I went for £40,000, a record in those days for full-backs – could've bought bloody Sla'wit for that!

Mel Booth

sports writer for the Huddersfield Daily Examiner

I'm local, born in Cartworth Moor, so a Holmfirth lad and a Town supporter all my life. I've been a reporter of their exploits since 1985. I supported them through school, Holme Valley School (now Honley High) and saw my first match in 1967. After leaving school I qualified in journalism and started work for the *Holme Valley Express* and the *Huddersfield & District Chronicle*, then I went to the *Colne Valley Chronicle* and on to the *Barnsley Chronicle* for a couple of years in sport. After that I went on to the *Morning Telegraph* in Sheffield until it was closed down. I came here in 1985 and have been covering Town fortunes, plus cricket, ever since. I still play cricket for Scholes CC. I'm no relation of the Huddersfield Town hero, Andy Booth, but we play in the same league. Andrew's a very good cricketer.

The high spots as a Town reporter, to date, have been the 1994/95 seasons. It was a bit special as the club had qualified to go to

Mel Booth.

Wembley for the first time since before the Second World War, fifty-six years in fact. It created a huge stir around the town though it was only the Autoglass Trophy, as it was then known – there have been various guises since. It was a big thrill because folk a lot older then me had not had the chance to see Huddersfield Town play at Wembley yet they were acutely aware of the club's great history. Arriving there on the day with the team was amazing, just a sea of blue and white everywhere. There didn't appear to be many Swansea Town fans around, just a huge bank of ours facing us. We lost the game but having suffered such disappointment to go back and win promotion the following season was wonderful. So, those two years were terrific and I will always cherish them.

There have been disappointments, of course: losing two play-offs, in '92 against the Posh and then against Brentford. The loss of the old Leeds Road ground was inevitable, upkeep had been very expensive and the stadium was decaying rapidly. Memories of Leeds Road though were fabulous, particularly for older folk who naturally became very attached to the place. It was a big, old-style ground with a terrific atmosphere. At the end there was a mixture of pride and melancholy as the club went from the old to the new. The crowds have doubled, if 6,000 attended the old ground it would have been special indeed. Town were looking forward hopefully to being a 20,000 crowd club: the facilities are undeniably there but it's a rocky road.

The stadium has undeniably given the town an identity. People who know it for nothing else know it for the stadium. I think it's great to look across from the Riverside to the Kilner Bank with its magnificent tree-covered backdrop. How many grounds could boast anything like it? It's really wonderful.

There have been some memorable characters. I was in contact with Dennis Law to get him on to help lay the centre plaque from the old Leeds Road ground, now in the retail park. Dennis came over and told me that he had sat next to Bill Shankly, Town's manager, in the stand at Charlton during that fantastic match. He said it was the most incredible game of football he had ever seen. He couldn't believe what was happening. It's still a record, the only top division team to score six goals and lose, a source of pride as well as angst for the Town.

Steve Kinder was very popular as a player when he came into Mick Buxton's team in '69/70. He always chased lost causes, got people excited, and has done the same as commercial manager when he finished playing. He had organized a forty-mile walk to the first match of the season in 1984 at Blackburn. They set off the previous day, walking over the hills with Steve in front like the Pied Piper dragging the rest behind him. They actually arrived at half time and the crowd gave them a standing ovation as they marched down the tunnel and around the edge of the pitch. I think the match was symbolically a draw. Steve was never off the phone, he always had something interesting to say about Town.

There have been others: Neil Warnock was a terrific bloke to deal with. Now at Sheffield United he was another one who appreciated how much football meant to people in the area. He offered us a column which he would tape every week and it was very popular. Peter Jackson, I have to say, is a really, really great guy, very caring of the football club. As a player he wore his heart on his sleeve and as the manager he is exactly the same. Let's face it, he started his return season with only eight players, we could barely field a five-a-side team yet we achieved promotion.

David Green

publican and Huddersfield's pub historian

Bentley & Shaw Brewery

Timothy Bentley was born about 1767 and started brewing in Warley, near Halifax. He moved to Meltham Mills and then finally to Lockwood, to pure spring water with its advantages to brewing at Horse Bank Spring. Those were the days of the alehouses, not beerhouses, on the pack-horse routes over the hills, and the coaching inns. The yeast ferments at the top in ale and at the bottom in beer to which hops are added. The 'Cart & Horse' and the 'Plough' were examples from the mid-1700s, before Bentley was born.

The old Isle of Skye, up on the Saddleworth road, was a Seth Senior house, which came under an Act of the Huddersfield Corporation. Unusually, Timothy Bentley managed to acquire twenty-six acres of freehold land at Lockwood, Lockwood Park, as it was called. It didn't belong to the Ramsdens, who were the landowners of Huddersfield and who put everything out on a lease. Bentley managed it through what we might call 'Yorkshire negotiation', for the Ramsdens owned virtually all the land from Almondbury to Holmfirth and Marsden. The borough, when it was formed in 1868, was one mile in circumference and excluded Sheepridge, Bradley and Lindley cum Quarmby, part of which was in Halifax in those days. There was a pub up at Ainley, the Green Stile, and there were arguments in there in the 1860s as to whose jurisdiction it lay in.

When the beerhouses were created in July 1830 there was straight-line thinking as to how they should be rated. Magistrates were much exercised by rates. Alehouses were different because inns and taverns offered food and accommodation, especially the inns. Beerhouses were simply nothing more than ordinary houses turned by invitation of the government into houses selling beer. People had to submit a plan and be vetted by the JP as to their fitness and propriety. They were very unpretentious places, rated at £14-16 per year, with flagged floors and there was a definite 'want of cleanliness'.

The infamous loos

We have to remember that there was no street lighting and the only light in pubs was from tallow candles. There was little comfort, seating was primitive, certainly no cushions, and there were no toilets, a facility we naturally take for granted today. Hence the saying, 'going round/out the back'. The ladies had to be crafty: they wore long skirts, of course, and were obliged, as charmingly as possible, to gracefully curtsy. The men had to be as bad, have a friend put a 'robe' around the three-quarter coat having nipped up the back, where everything went into the gutter.

1,477ft ASL: the Isle of Skye on Meltham Moor. (D. Green)

There's a tale of a publican who tested his apprentice's honesty by leaving money about the place. He left it on the shelf and later on the floor. On each occasion the lad gave him it back but he still continued to really try and test the poor lad by putting a two guinea piece in a corner he knew collected dust. The money never came back so when the lad was going home the publican quizzed him. 'Did you find anything on the floor when you were sweeping up?' 'No', said the lad, 'I put it all on t'shovel and threw it in t' gutter'. 'Course, the gutters took everything. The chap, fuming, was obliged to get on his hands and knees and rummage through the muck. He found his coin but he never said a word to the lad again. It's said that there was a pub up at Golcar where the landlord charged his customers 1s 6d a year to keep the outside 'loos' in repair. After the 1920s pubs were improved considerably, some being pulled down and built again, including The Black Lion on Upper Head Row. It had been known as the 'Hum', a name earned by its infamous toilet facilities. A toilet was installed in 1922.

The dispensing was also a mixed bag, the beer being piped from wherever the barrel landed through a mixture of all sorts of telescopic attachments, a lot of it lead. The amount of beer sold was prodigious. One place of refreshment in town declared itself bankrupt in around 1870 yet in the cellar were four hogsheads of bitter (fifty-four gallons apiece), ten times thirty-six gallons of pale ale and a couple of eighteens, and they said they were going bankrupt.

It's interesting to see how quickly people latched on to change. There's a story from 21 May, 1885, at the 'Bull & Mouth', which stood at the back of where the library is now. They had Vienna Lager on draught in those days. They said 'objectionable lead piping was entirely dispensed with', so they were aware of the problems associated with lead even at a time when most of the water-supply piping was still lead. This, of course, was an up-market pub, the chap who owned it was twice mayor of Huddersfield, one James Albert Woolvens.

Bentley & Shaw was, of course, the principal brewer in Huddersfield and Timothy Bentley, who died while on jury service in York, was buried in the crypt in Queen Street Mission. A story, which may be true, said that when he was later reinterred the body was found to be in excellent condition when refurbishment took place in the early 1870s. Well, what might this be attributable to? In the early 1800s there was plague in Huddersfield and the Mission was used as a burial chamber: the cellars were rather like a bakery with slots where they'd lay the bodies, little ones for the children. Tim's good state is a mystery. When he died in 1830 he owned eleven pubs in Huddersfield and his brewery could produce 350 x 36 gallon barrels a week. Mind, not like Bass, in 1850 they were doing 350,000 barrels a year but that was in Burton-on-Trent where the brewers had the railways organized to deliver all over the country, including Huddersfield.

In the nineteenth century in the up-market establishments the clientele were gentlemen. Like the George Hotel, the

Site of the Bentley & Shaw Brewery. Now used for other purposes.

The Bull & Mouth. (D. Green)

birthplace of rugby league, which was moved to the station because the railway had arrived, the 'George Inn', which stood in the market place, was taken down brick by brick and put in St Peter's Street – Temple Street – when the station arrived in July 1847. Similarly, the Druids' Hotel was taken apart stone by stone and put in Ramsden Street where in recent years it became an Irish theme pub, 'O'Neill's'. It was originally named The Zetland or Marquis of Zetland. It may have reverted to that or something similar.

After the Second World War, Bentley & Shaw was quite an aggressive brewery, looking to have a house on every street corner selling pints of their beer. There's a story of a chap coming back from an ale prize gathering in London saying to another chap in the offices of Bentley & Shaw that they could be agents for a new drink imported from America. In blunt Yorkshire dialect, the chap in the office said, 'We're brewers, not soft drink merchants'. It transpired that the drink he'd shown scant respect for was Coca Cola. The benefit of foresight might have instructed him otherwise.

Tim Bentley's best drink was 'Bentley's Old', much favoured by the local Victorian Societies such as the Druids, the Oddfellows, the Gardeners, the Dog Owners Club, the Hedge Growers – they loved it.

When landlords applied for licences to the magistrates, if they had lodge rooms in their houses they were viewed very favourably. The term 'house' has long gone but you were in fact drinking in somebody's front room. Public houses are about people. How many other countries have tried to copy English pubs but they can't run 'em right.

The Zetland.

The average man in the street would never appreciate that the public house has its own laws. People go into pubs and they start moving your furniture about. Why don't they ask? Somebody comes in, goes straight to your fire and turns it off. 'Excuse me, what are you doing?' 'I'm too warm'. 'What about everybody else in the house, are they too warm? If we came into your house and did what you're doing, what would you say?' The answer would be obvious. Also, there's the argument. In the local community pub the word would be said, the argument and the fight erupt … in somebody else's house.

Police nowadays talk about binge drinking but nothing's ever altered. The controlling of ale consumption has always been a problem, as much so today as it's ever been. In 1868 they brought in the Sunday law and another one forbidding the sale of beer between midnight and four in the morning. From 1845 onwards they've tried to introduce controlling laws. Before that you could drink beer at any time. People resent restriction and refuse to adhere to it. We once had a bloke from Los Angeles in The Slubbers and when we called last orders he called it 'cute'. We brought all those laws in to control drinking and it's like prohibition, it's actually made it worse. There have been thousands of occurrences when publicans have been brought before the magistrate for serving during prohibited hours – there were five offences: pulling, filling, consuming, drinking, allowing.

There used to be a law prohibiting dominoes. A landlord at Birkby was fined for 'permitting and suffering the playing of dominoes in his house' without a licence. The only lawful game was cribbage as

The Slubbers Arms.

it was deemed to be a game of skill. Nowadays, you can gamble to a certain extent without the landlord's permission but how many people actually ask permission?

There were fifteen-plus beerhouses in 1957 and they were all encouraged to apply for full licences but there was a red herring in the application. The value of the house as a beerhouse was taken, then its value as it closed down, and finally the value as though it had been granted a full licence and the overall differences between the three was taken from the value of the actual sale as a fully licensed property. The final tally was called 'monopoly money' and this had to paid to gain the full licence. It cost The Slubbers £958 in 1958.

The seamy side

Times had changed as the beerhouses were for men and one or two 'ladies'. On the other hand, it's amazing how many ladies did keep pubs in Huddersfield. At the top end of town a lot of pubs were disguised brothels. There was a pub, 'The Friendly', down Lower End Row, which is now Old Leeds Road. The licensing authority set up a watch committee to judge the houses on how they were being conducted. The landlord and lady had spent eighteen and twelve months respectively in the house of correction at Wakefield for allowing their house to be used as a brothel. When they were both released they applied for their licence and when they turned up in court he was drunk so on the first day the magistrate wouldn't listen to him. In the meantime a gentleman from the watch committee went to look at his house and when he entered he noticed

David in action in the Slubbers Arms. (D. Green)

that the house contained, 'persons of undesirable character...and other means', some of the lower end of the town life. When he went upstairs he found a man in bed with two ladies, a little bit of Huddersfield troilism, in 1858. Needless to say, the licence was refused.

Another story concerned The Bold Venture in Kirkgate, which as a street had more pubs than any other in town. A young lady working there as a servant was told by the landlady that giving hospitality to gentlemen customers was just that. After eight weeks she'd contracted syphilis, spent eight weeks on rest cure and was then back to work. In another pub for every shilling the girls earned, the landlord took 4d. There was a house in the Beast Market run by a Thomas Styring who was a cab proprietor, a wine and spirit merchant as well as a publican. He was fined in 1869 for allowing 'young ladies to gather and assemble, taking far too long over their refreshments and following through' in his house. Don't you just love the understated Victorian expression.

Ron Crabtree outside his brewhouse, The Sair.

In the 1800s most houses were Free Houses: you could buy from any brewery of your choice. A lot, indeed, were home brew, of which there are growing number, including The Sair at Linthwaite and The Star down at Folly Hall. The former had been the New Inn: the new name was local dialect for sour.

A chap called Aquila Priestley had a pub on the old Halifax Road called 'The Noah's Ark' and it looked like an old wash kitchen. He led the revolt against The Ramsden Leasing Act and it got to the House of Commons but Ramsden was the landowner. Brewers wouldn't give up properties and he wouldn't give up the lease, which was increased from 99 to 999 years. The Ramsden Estate Office was where Tailor Quigley's, if it's still called that, is now. It was the HQ of the Huddersfield Liberal Association for along time. The side entrance led to a top-notch gentlemen's club in the same building. The entrance, in Railway Street, is still full of polished marble. You can imagine the horse-drawn carriages with the immaculately dressed drawing up at the place. That dates back to the 1870s and membership was five guineas a year, a considerable sum.

In 1920 Huddersfield Corporation bought the Ramsden estate for £1.2 million. There are still some Ramsdens and Bentleys about, probably from the less affluent of the families. You also get tangents of these families who were wealthy, particularly some millionaires who kept tied houses. The owner might take a shine to a wife or daughter and the tenants were too afraid to say anything.

The Old Ramsden Estate Offices.

So, when you do the family tree with nine children and one or two other 'children', you have to decide who daddy was. Certain mill owners were renowned for it. One in particular: when a new girl started he came to 'inspect' and sometimes succeeded. Money and power were a telling combination. There was one in our family tree, one from Honley.

Mrs Sunderland

There's the lovely story of Mrs Sunderland, founder of the internationally famous music competition. She was born a Miss Sykes about 1819 and she died in the 1890s. She was always a singer; at sixteen she appeared in 'The Ramsden's Arms Glee and Madrigal Society' giving a concert in the pub. She was renowned for her precise singing. She lived in Brighouse at the time and she used to walk to Huddersfield. Sounds hard but it was quite common at a time when people used to walk ten miles to work, do a hard day and then walk back again.

So, Mrs Sunderland used to attract a lot of people to sing at Huddersfield Town Hall, Bradford, and Brighouse, and she was also very friendly with James Hirst, who was the organist at Slaithwaite parish church for many years. He also kept The Harp Inn, next door to the church. She was also a friend of Ephraim Wood who kept The Lewisham Hotel. Of course, being a musical house, with the name Harp Inn, musicians were always encouraged to come and sing. She used to go to Slaithwaite regularly to sing in both houses. The Lewisham was pulled down in the 1960s. Long before that Ephraim Wood wrote that international favourite 'Roses of Picardy'. Opposite Huddersfield police station you'll find a plaque to a Mr Parrott, born in Spring Street, who was Queen Victoria's musician and organist. The Huddersfield area has always been musically so strong, particularly choral.

The Victorians were very, very good at entertaining themselves. They loved gardens and were famous promenaders. There were five pubs in Huddersfield that had rhododendron gardens, walkways and tea dances. A chap called Potter who kept The Pomona Hotel at Dalton was also a firework manufacturer who toured the country giving displays. His family would run the hotel from *c.* 1832 to *c.* 1916. He had bloom walks and tea dances, the 'fat man and thin lady', penny farthing rides and acrobats in his establishment. On a Monday night it was 1d to go in, at weekends 2d. On a bank holiday there'd be 2,500 people there and you'd find much the same in the valleys of Golcar and Linthwaite. On a bank holiday everybody went to the valleys and moors on the edge of town for entertainment. Hope Bank at Honley was known as 'the Blackpool of the North'. The bank had a boating lake, fairground, and rides of all kinds – it was a real day out. It's all gone now, buried under Brook Motors, as was. There were also the Marsh House Gardens and the Shakespeare Gardens at Marsh, now all gone under housing. Up at Sheepridge were the Bellevue Gardens of Mr Aspinall. Wonderful gardens and a bowling green, all gone under new residential development. Holmfirth had its Fearnought Gardens and its Lido, which survived until the 1930s. The gardens and the promenading was the venue for folk meeting in a respectable manner really until the 1870/80s as moods and fashions changed. On the maps, of course, all these licensed houses with their wonderful names are not shown as such: they were classed as shops. Only The Pomona appeared because it was a beer garden.

Mrs Sunderland. (Kirklees Archive)

Boating lake, Hope Bank, Honley, early twentieth century. (Peter Bray)

They'd also gather round the piano in the pub lodge rooms. In the more updated establishments like The Cherry Tree, The Green Dragon, The Star and The George Inn you'd find all sorts. Henry Ellis, the landlord of the George, encouraged a building society complete with articles, associations and shares which were published in the paper, so you could buy and sell them. So, you'd get such as the following, 'At the home of Mr Bottomley at seven o'clock on the third Monday of every month, when the Cloth Hall clock strikes seven, the meeting shall commence. Discussion of shares, payments and collections will be available upon request'. As the Friendly Societies were the forerunners of Savings Clubs, providing health insurance, benefits upon death and penny policies, so the building societies encouraged the development of houses. What they'd do, the up-and-coming workers, was pay in and if/when they could afford it they'd apply to the pub building society for a mortgage.

Pubs and morality

The decent and otherwise have always had to cohabit in the pub business and that brings to mind another story. A young lady, a well-educated lass, came from The Junction at Golcar to play in a pub on Upper Head Row. She'd played a couple of times when a gentleman approached her with an indecent suggestion. She went to the landlady about it. She reportedly replied, 'Never mind dear, second room on the right upstairs'. The young lady obviously did whatever was required of her as the gentleman parted with 6d, which the landlady took. The 'suggestion' led to about a dozen visits to this room and each time the landlady took the 6d. In the end the young lady was so disgruntled that she reported the matter to the police. The magistrates fined the landlord and lady and removed their licence. Another chap was recommended to take over the pub upon which it started all over again – business as usual. Stories like that never go amiss.

There were certainly two degrees in Victorian society and to an extent they were hypocrites. Like modern political correctness, in those days there was 'Victorian face', one life at home and another away. There was never a shortage of ladies to be disadvantaged and so many of them were desperately poor. The workforce was oppressed and kept at a level that ensured that they would always do the main thing required of them, turn up for work. More than enough mill owners took pubs themselves so they could take back the pittance they'd given out.

Ale then was 1d a pint and it was all strong stuff, 6 per cent ABV. The excise duty was just on malt in those days, on how much was used in production. In the 1860s there were thirty-two brewers in Huddersfield plus the home brewers. There were take outs, pins of four and a half gallons as special deliveries as well as the normal pub trade. In suburban villages like Honley and Meltham, Bentley & Shaw had a near monopoly, which passed on when they were taken over by Hammonds in 1944, later Charringtons in 1962, which finally disappeared into Bass in 1970. Beer, like car registration, lost its local flavour.

There was a chap actually called Bentley Shaw, which is how the firm got the name by which it is generally known, Bentley & Shaw. Timothy's daughter married one William Shaw, who became part of the family and who actually ran the brewery at Lockwood. Their son, born 1830, was christened Bentley. He died about 1878 having been a magistrate, JP and the owner of a couple of pubs. He'd have spent some time prosecuting his customers, lecturing them about inappropriate conduct and then expect them to go back and buy his ale.

Records

Huddersfield is a bit short of records as the county town was Wakefield, which is where the records were sent. For some strange reason when Huddersfield became the seat of Kirklees Metropolitan Council the records of public houses were 'misplaced'. What happened, we don't know. Maybe somebody does. After 1868, when Huddersfield became a borough, everyone was instructed to keep better records. Every house had a fully detailed file in the records, now it's all gone. To find any record in Wakefield you need a reference number but these in turn can be a mystery.

It's been interesting and infuriating trying to track down such records as are out there somewhere. Pubs were the focal point in the lives of some many people. You might say that what they didn't get or find at home they found in the pub. It isn't until you keep a pub that you realize how many lonely people there are. Many people simply cannot cope with being on their own.

Gruesome insights

Pubs also acted as law courts and mortuaries. The unfortunates from fatal accidents in the mills were often laid out in pubs. The more gruesome the better, of course, much like rubbernecking on motorways today. If somebody was wrapped up in the weaving machine they'd take them, bits and all in a

The Royal, Milnsbridge.

bucket, and lay them out. There was a story of two girls at The Dolphin House, now 'The Royal' in Milnsbridge. The two lasses had been a bit adventurous one night with two lads while their parents had gone on an outing to Brighouse. Possibly in a fit of remorse, they threw themselves into the canal. The crowd had to queue outside the pub in order to see the bodies while thousands more stood at the death scene. This was, of course, before the infirmary was built by Joseph Kaye. Thus the changes were rung.

As for law courts, The Black Bull at Birstall, for example, had a lodge room upstairs, which served as a court. When they gave the death sentence, the unfortunate was marched downstairs and hanged from a tree in the garden – didn't put the customers off their ale.

An entertaining skirmish with Alan Chapman

hairdresser and much-loved raconteur, together with Alan Driscoll, customer and retired journalist

From the depths of Bradford I started hairdressing over here and I've been very happy. I was two doors up to start with and gradually worked my way down here. This place was a flat at the time; when it came up for sale it saved me paying me rent on the other place. Before it was a flat it'd been a pub, The Westgate Arms. Very small, obviously, and we've still got the old gantries down in the cellar. I bought the place from a chap called George Hobson, who was known as 'Trappem'. He had pigeon lofts on the roof and 'twas rumoured he used to trap other people's birds and sell 'em in the pub. A right character. I first met him in the Con Club and introduced myself. 'Hello, I'm Alan Chapman. You're Mr Trappem, are you?' I thought it were his name and he wasn't over pleased. (One of Alan's lady clients interjected, 'I've been coming 'ere for t'last thirty-two years. You come 'ere to get insulted' – howls of laughter). I can always recollect how long I've been here as my wife was pregnant with our daughter at the time. Fruit of the loins, eh? Weren't married at the time and in those days it was still a bit risque so we had to tie the knot fairly rapidly.

I remember the time when I was pulled up by a copper for driving on the newly made pedestrian precinct. He gave me a ticket to produce me documents at the nearest police station, Holmfirth nick. Sunday teatime I took the documents up there. Copper behind the counter said, 'OK, fine, fine. How've you got 'ere? You live in Meltham?' I said, 'I've come in the car.' 'Oh 'ave you, there's a strong smell of alcohol, sir. Would you mind blowing into this?' I parked me car up and virtually surrendered meself. It was Sunday afternoon, I'd 'ad a couple of bevvies, it was my wife's fortieth birthday, 18 January. I rang her up and said you'd better ring and cancel the restaurant. She asked why, I said I'm in prison. It was January and bloody cold outside. It were even colder when I got 'ome and met the icy blast. Not many go'n surrender, eh? 'Excuse me officer, I've been drinking, can you breathalyze me please?' Well, desk sergeant were alright, it'd been their Christmas do a couple of nights before so I got some mince pies with me cuppa.

Alan's tireless support of leukaemia research

I got into research when a local lad died of leukaemia. We had a committee going, a fairly small group in those days but we've gone from strength to strength. I've been involved for about thirty years. In the very first year we raised £50, last year we raised over £2,000. This year with our sponsored parachute jumps it'll be even more. Jumping out of a plane has to be the first outrageous thing I've done since surrendering meself ... and getting married. And I've got a strange window cleaner. That's enough to qualify me for being bloody stupid; I might even pay him this week.

In the air for leukaemia research. (A. Chapman)

Made it! (A. Chapman)

Honley Lib. Did Churchill stand up there?

Alan Driscoll, a retired journalist, was having his hair cut by Alan while the conversation was in progress. He's seventy-seven years old and had been a journalist with the *Huddersfield Daily Examiner*. 'The influence of Methodism has been profound in choral music and the vast array of biblical names used in the valleys, e.g. Ephraim, Esau, Josiah, Jedediah. Not popular these days of course'. 'Talking of names, a local one that lends itself is Hoyle when you think on if you've summat appropriate stood in front like Wood or Key' (Alan C). 'One of the favourite confrontations I ever had was on a London 'do'. Four or five us from the West Riding papers used to go down to these fairs and one of them was a member of the National Liberal Club and he elected to get us in there. I remember its library was one the finest in London and we were happy to stay there overnight. We got up for breakfast and went to the lift, one of its quainter features. We just got to the gates when this great giant of a figure came at me from the other side. Had we collided at the gates he'd have knocked me flying. It was, of course, none other than Cyril Smith. One of the most famous political figures of his day, he was a real bigwig in his native Rochdale, did a lot for the town' (Alan D).

'This area was very strong for the Liberal party, going back before its most revered MP, Richard Wainwright; a candidate here was Lady Violet Bonham-Carter. I believe I'm right in saying that she was some relation of Gladstone and, anyway, one of the Liberal pioneers. She was a great friend of Winston Churchill and he came up to support her candidature, even though he was a Conservative. I'm almost certain he appeared with her on the balcony of the Lib Club in Honley before a massive crowd. The only time, I think, he came to Huddersfield' (Alan D). 'You usually find our local Liberal councillors in the Con Club, p'raps beer's better in there' (Alan C). 'I think you'd only ever see an official Conservative representative at the Con Club once in the blue moon at an election time. Don't think the rest of 'em dare come' (Alan D).

'Years ago though, when George Kaye was involved with the politics, he was a Labour candidate, standing for the party, and couldn't understand it when the Con Club refused him membership. He preferred the Con Club even while he was standing for the Labour Party but in those days the clubs were much more politically oriented. His wife, who died recently, was the District Nurse, much loved and remembered by all' (Alan C). 'There were a lot of people at her funeral where I recollected an interesting story about her. She used to travel around on a bike, up and down the Holme Valley in all sorts of weather. In the midst of winter on a truly dire day she was known to travel around with hot water bottles strapped to her person' (Alan D).

'We had a wonderful talk last week at the Civic Society. The speaker was a local historian who talked about the history of Honley, showing some maps going back to the 1500s. The place names are still the same and there's a story that the Scots passed through here on their way to Derby with Prince Charles Edward Stuart. The street called Sentry recalls somebody reputedly watching out for them – probably a yarn'. (One of the entries into the village, Scotgate, is thought to refer to this time but Scot was an old English word for tax, as in scot free or tax free. Gate was an actual road into a town or city. What we call a gate today was a bar, e.g. Micklegate Bar in the city of York). 'Unfortunately our resident expert with invaluable knowledge of the history of Fartown Rugby League (Huddersfield Giants) hasn't come in yet. He actually took it as a specialist subject for his O levels at school. He's called Robert ...among other things' (Alan C).

'I were just thinking about how cosmopolitan an area Huddersfield is. In my own family, my late wife and her sister Shirley were part Dutch, part English. Shirley married Bill Forbes, a pop singer of the late '50s/early '60s. He came from Sri Lanka, part Scottish, part Sri Lankan. They had two kids. Now Tracy's married a lad who's half-Hungarian. It's a great melting pot, is Huddersfield.

My customers are an interesting lot. One lass who was in earlier, she's from Brum and one of her brothers-in-law was a real character, in little bits of trouble with the law but nothing serious. The last thing he ever did, as far as I know, against the law was break into the Co-op and when the police arrived he didn't make any effort to run off. He was just sitting in the middle of the floor drinking beer from the shelves. He were real intelligent though, could tell anybody how to fill in their claim for the Soash (Social Security). He had a mate, used to call round and scrounge a pack of roll-up baccy from him, regular, this was. Anyhow, John, this lad, went to t' post office with a parcel addressed to himself for delivery next day, when t' other lad'd be visiting. He arrived and saw t' parcel on the step. 'John, you've a parcel 'ere'. 'Oh aye, that'll be me baccy from t' Soash'. 'Ya what?' 'Aye, Soash send me a parcel of free baccy every month'. The other lad hauled off to town and played merry 'ell with Soash for not sending him his free baccy.

Alan in festive ensemble. (A. Chapman)

Bill Parker

GP

We arrived as 'comers in' about 1950 when I was eighteen months old. My mum came to be senior mistress at Holme Valley Grammar School and dad looked for work. If you weren't born and raised locally in those days you were definitely a 'comer in' as it very tribal. There were no discipline problems at the grammar school. Eleven plus was required for entry and late starters might go a year behind. One of my mum's duties was to ensure that all female staff wore a hat on the way to school and that all staff wore collegiate gowns when teaching. She would sometimes come to school in Rupert's taxi – considered somewhat amazing and rather upper class. Rupert ran the taxi service for the valley in a London cab. One year we even hired him to take the family to Filey.

All the boys at Holme Valley Grammar School had to wear caps to school, even in the sixth form, and it was a caneable offence to be seen coming to or going from school without. You were caned by Mr Braine, whose fiery lady wife was the headmistress of the local prep school in Thongsbridge, which I attended. Thus, I've come a long way in my life, about 150 yards from the old school gates. Dad got various jobs in those days. He worked in the clerk's office when they built Digley reservoir. One day a fellow came in. ''I've come for me cards'. 'Why? You're a good man, a good worker.' 'I've come for me cards!' 'Why, tell me why'. 'Well, I were driving dumper on t' top of banking and it went over t'edge and I jumped off, dumper's lyin' at bottom'. My dad looked at him. 'Well, you'd better have your cards then.'

Dad was also very happy in the offices of the local steeplejacks, Tinker's, located in the main square in Huddersfield. Huddersfield was then stacked out with chimneys and Tinker's also looked after church spires. Chimneys had to clear the landscape to allow the smoke away. Rock Mill chimney at Brockholes was over 200ft high and that huge, magnificent chimney is still there in Armitage Bridge. Most were knocked down but some were blown up. Dad took me as a treat to see one being brought down with explosives. The story goes, maybe true, that Tinker's was founded when Tinker himself was seen climbing a chimney using its metal bands for purchase with his hooked ropes. The mill owner who witnessed this was sufficiently impressed to buy him some ladders.

I remember this as a woollen area creating much wealth for some: it was life and work for almost everybody. When I knew it as a youngster it was coming towards its end in the 1960s and '70s. Rock Mill alone, in its heyday, had 200 weavers. They tended to be local but labour had to be shipped in. The women came over from Barnsley, which was very much a male-dominated area with few jobs for women. They were bussed over to mend the cloth. The weaving sheds were noisy places and I still see a lot of old people

Digley Reservoir looking mysterious.

The dam wall at Digley.

with noise-induced deafness dating from those times. They could all lip read, and I remember Ethel who lived next door to my auntie. She had a dimple in the side of her temple where a shuttle had flown off the loom, glanced off the side of her head and buried itself in the nearby shed door.

The mill owners were rich and have left the legacy of large houses and they would not hesitate to use their own skilled workforce to do jobs in their own homes. One local joinery firm had one of its carpenters retained full-time by Josiah France for all of his working life. Indeed, the whole of the local economy tied in to the woollen industry. This is one of the reasons why engineering firms and the chemical industry developed in Huddersfield.

Most of the people I talk to look back on that world with a deal of happiness but one chap employed at the sewage works insisted that all they had to eat during the depression were pickled eggs – there were many tall stories.

Coming from a professional background I was one of the first kids to have a full-time childminder. My mother put an ad in the Co-op and a childless couple took me on. They became Auntie and Uncle and indeed like parents to me. They came from the working-class West Riding background of big families. My uncle's dad was the last man in the valley to die of typhoid. I got to know both of their large extended families and their Yorkshire ways and this has stood me in good stead throughout my life. My uncle was eighty-four when he died, auntie was seventy-two. She was a woman with a 'fighting weight' of twenty-one stone and only 5ft 3in., magnificent folk and very talented people. Auntie was an excellent singer and she could automatically sing hymns in descant without even thinking about it. When the weavers at the mill felt aggrieved and headed for the office, Flo was up front and the guy at the office would say, 'Now then Flo, what's up lass?' as they stood in serried ranks, arms akimbo, accepting no nonsense. She'd collect her pay at one booth and go to the next to pay the rent. They had a cellar kitchen below ground level, a room on the ground floor and two bedrooms upstairs. In the attic they had a loom where they did those rag rugs which lasted for years. Anyone wanting them would kneel on the pavement and knock on the cellar window.

The valley was a lovely place but quite different from now: it was black with soot, walls, grass alike. If you stood on the hillside you couldn't see Huddersfield as the whole area was covered by a pall of smoke. If it rained on washday Monday there was panic. Folk rushed to retrieve their washing as the rain brought masses of soot and smoke back to earth very rapidly. The only time we had a remotely clean atmosphere was during textile fortnight in summer when the whole place closed for holidays. It would work like that in the north of England so that places like Blackpool, Scarborough, Brid and Morecambe could cope with the influxes from various places in the industrial area.

In my time there was only one boy who came to school and still played football in his clogs yet I remember wearing them. They were very comfortable and warm but the clog irons on the bottom would gather mud and snow. October half term was potato picking week when kids helped the farmers to get their spuds in. The teacher at Bird's Edge School, when we were living in Upper Cumberworth, would say, 'Now then children, who's earned sixpence potato picking? Some of them earned half a crown, they must have worked very, very hard'. I played all day long but many of the kids were obliged to go picking, this was in the

1950s. They were happy days at school, if you did anything wrong you picked your own slipper, yet slipperings were few and usually well deserved.

The first doctor I met was Dr Johnson in Honley. I went to prep school with his daughter, Jane. I was not a natural scholar but fortunately discovered biology, which opened a wholly wonderful new world. Other subjects were very, very difficult. Initially, I applied for agricultural college but my dad suggested that I wouldn't like earning money for someone else. The penny dropped and I sought medicine with its six years of training. I went to Birmingham where one of the interviewers questioned my roots asking, 'Do you think Birmingham is far enough north for you?' I qualified in 1971; Birmingham had been good. Then it was a decision between British Columbia and Huddersfield, the latter winning out because of the roots connection. There was no GP training scheme in those days. You could get a job in the local hospital and look around for a practice amenable to both parties. I rang up the hospital secretary at the HRI and asked if there were any jobs going for a senior house officer. He said, 'We've three specialisations which are vacant'. So, I did six months obstetrics, came to HRI and met Mr Dennis who really didn't know what to ask me at the interview and we agreed to start whenever I wished to. I worked in a very hard job at HRI, delivering twins, breeches, ectopic pregnancies – very hard but hey, I enjoyed it.

I remember when Deirdre Cashin, my partner, moved into Honley. 'Did you know', she said, 'our seventeen year-old childminder is one you delivered?' I had a guy come down the surgery and he said, 'Me mum said to tell you that you delivered me'. I said, 'Yeah, I think you were a breech'. We had our children delivered at HRI. I remember I delivered one large lady, we had started her off because her BP was going up. She delivered a breech, a nice baby and a good size. I was beginning to put the stitches in when she said, 'I want to push'. We told her to be quiet but suddenly there was another bulging membrane pushing at me. I said, 'Bloody hell, there's another'. Hey presto, I ruptured the membrane and out it came. It was about the time my wife delivered so her post-natal visit coincided with the mother and her twins. She, the mother, was sitting in the waiting area regaling the whole room with the tale of this little curly-haired doctor saying, 'Bloody hell, here's another'.

My second job was in psychiatry in the modern, state-of-the-art unit at St Luke's Hospital. Storthes Hall Hospital, an old-style asylum in the country, was still operating and like all the asylums in the land it was a throwback to another age. 'Fallen women' had been admitted to these places and it was not unknown that if an unmarried girl became pregnant her mental health was questioned. The age of these asylums had now passed. They were bankrupting the health authorities and that was one of the major reasons for their closure. The introduction of drugs was the other. Chlorpromazine was the principal drug for controlling schizophrenia and mania, enabling biochemical rather than institutional control. A lot of people were now able to live in the community and be helped there. Of course, there was the gradual realization that keeping people in an institution didn't make them better, it made them worse. People clung on to these fixed beliefs; when I visited one asylum as a medical student, I remember the superintendent being approached by the head gardener who pleaded with him not to discharge so and so, as he was one of the best gardeners he had and would, by virtue of his industry, be irreplaceable. So, we were emerging from the dark ages really. When the asylums closed it cost more per capita to look after somebody in the community and we are still, today, trying to come to terms with the financial implications of looking after the mentally ill. There have certainly been one or two horror stories of patients being inadequately supported in inappropriate accommodation.

On a lighter side, my old boss loved the Holme Valley; he had many patients here. He liked to consider the geography of the place and he said that if you put a wall around the edge of the valley, right up to Holme Moss, and then roofed it over you could possibly call it an asylum – just joking. The gist of his argument was that there was so much individuality that is rooted in and continued from the past, in particular, the independence that women were given in the woollen industry. If you were a weaver, you had to think, you didn't work in a line in a supervised gang. You really had to have independence of thought. Before that you had that dogged hill stock and I'm sure that John Wesley recognized this and they recognized him as an independent free thinker. So, there was no tribal male dominance as there was in other areas. There is a local tradition that the first chapel in the West Riding in which Wesley preached was behind The Cricketers pub in Netherthong. It's now converted into a house. When he came over the hill he said, 'A wilder people

Storthes Hall. (Kirklees Archive)

in England I have never seen in my life'. Dr Johnson, when I worked with him, said that in his early professional years he could recognize the cry of children with TB and meningitis. It was a differently pitched tone – they all died. Of course, there were fever hospitals and sanatoriums, all long gone as things have improved so much.

Just at the back of The Cricketers lay Deanhouse workhouse where St Mary's Estate is now. There was a fever and geriatric hospital there. Dick Turner, the father-in-law of a friend of mine, was a handyman and groundsman there. He had a horse, which towed a little snowplough around the ground in winter and generally dragged what needed dragging. Bob, my friend, was courting Dick's daughter, Marie, when this very large horse put a very large boot on Bob's foot. As he tried to pull his foot away the pressure increased, and again. Dick looked down and said, 'Hey, stop making fun of him. Take your foot off'. The horse had been playing a joke with Bob's foot. I think, probably, the horse summed up the rest of the population of the valley.

There were some fabulous characters. The Holmfirth bobby, whose wife still goes in The Cricketers, kept the town in good order. You'd get a whack of his cape, if necessary. When the navvies came down on a Friday night from building the reservoir, he'd count them off the bus and then count them all back on again. He wouldn't let the bus go until they were all rounded up and accounted for.

The railway goes through Brockholes and the *South Yorkshireman* used to stop at every little station from Bradford, through Huddersfield and all the way up to Penistone, Sheffield and then on to London. As kids we used to watch for it, looking for its name emblazoned on the front of the engine. Then the age of steam passed and in came the little trains we have now. When I left school I had a baptism of fire making drainage pipes in Denby Dale, and I thoroughly enjoyed it. It was an eye-opener to see what work was really like. I used to catch the train at 6.20 in the morning, there'd only be about three of us and the train was always run by a Sikh conductor. One day I was about ten minutes late and I ran up the hill thinking 'not a chance' but when I got there the train was still standing and the conductor said, 'I was only going to wait for another couple of minutes'. That was 1965, it wouldn't happen today.

After the war, Huddersfield soaked up immigrants to fill the demand for labour and I can well remember the early Pakistani migrants. You would never see a woman on the street in Lockwood, they would run into any available doorway. Now there has been a tremendous change with integration and the self-assured Sikh and Muslim young men and women, born in Huddersfield and all with their Yorkshire accent. The Poles, lots of them, came to Huddersfield. The Polish community was a fair size and Dr Grebecki looked after them. When he retired Dr Mohendron, an Indian doctor, took on the list, and he said to me one day, 'Bill, here I am from India and I'm looking after a lot of elderly ladies in headscarves from the middle of Europe who can hardly speak any English. How has it happened?' I said, 'I'm sure you'll manage'. It is a mix and just like anything else it strengthens the bloodlines.

After completing psychiatry I went to Brighouse for four and a half years but we always came back to Honley. One Friday afternoon, on the steps of the local butcher's, my children's godparents' shop, there was Mrs Johnson, who enjoyed significant status as a doctor's wife. She'd come from the chemist with a bar of soap she'd requested.

The ladies in the queue behind her took note and ordered the same. Well, she said, 'Oh Bill, I wish you were still living in Honley because we're looking for a fourth doctor as we're expanding the practice'. I replied, 'Oh don't worry about living in Honley'. By the following Tuesday I had the job, came to Honley and have never regretted it.

On my first home visit I went to an old codger on West Avenue. He looked at me, 'I asked for t' bloody doctor, not apprentice'. I told him I was the only doctor he was going to see that day and he'd have to make the best of it. There were some characters. Ephraim, a farmer, would go on holiday occasionally and he'd sell a cow to do so. In those days, up above on t'moor, as they called it, you'd find your typical hill farmhouse, a small place with a barn connected by a through door. I remember a trip up to one such house, a farmer had his coal delivered for the winter. Several tons of it dumped down in the middle of the barn, dust everywhere and totally ignored. He could easily access it without having to go outside from his kitchen.

1978 was a rotten winter: thankfully I was young then and I used to change the mini's wheels for the heavier winter version to get up the hills, but if there was enough snow it just bottomed and the sump would bury itself. One day I was digging it out when the milkman came up towing his milk on a trailer behind a tractor. I ended up being towed behind the trailer. I had a nice little parking slot outside what used to be Angus Pogson's shop and I can remember it banked up with snow all around. Sometimes you just had to walk.

On other occasions my butcher friends had one of the very few four-wheel drive vehicles in the valley and I used to sleep on their front room carpet and would be wakened by a very cheerful Dave at 5.30 in the morning. God knows why he got up at that time of the morning. When they finished their rounds or if there was an emergency I'd have their Land Rover. We'd go round and pick up the district nurses and see two blind diabetics who needed their insulin, inevitably drive into a snowdrift, back it out and carry on.

Respect and disrespect were dished out to me in varying amounts. I can remember caps being doffed to me as I walked down the street, which made me feel quite uncomfortable. On the other hand I can remember the practice manager saying, 'Well, you're not a bad doctor but I don't like your ways'. Hey, they're fairly blunt around here. One of the receptionists said she hadn't time to make me a cup of tea: she lasted six months. Some people find the local frankness rather abrasive; they do tend to call a spade a bloody shovel. I do the same at times. Folk have their 'familiar' doctors and folk are never slow in coming forward. Walking down from my home to the surgery I've had up to five consultations on the way by the time I reached the surgery door, but it never deterred me. Now it's much, much busier and we've no time to walk.

When I started as a GP my duty was to get people to three score years and ten: anything over that was a bonus. Now, you want to get the men to their late seventies and the women into their mid-eighties, with a good quality of life, not just surviving into old age. We seem now, however, to have more cancers. People are living longer with them or they survive after other illnesses only to get cancer. So, we appear to be surrounded by illness but what percentage of the population is over sixty?

Now we are into the ethical dilemma of keeping people alive and not being seen to hasten their end. If you're actually in the job it's more straightforward but the pressures are tremendous, particularly post-Shipman. An injection for anything has to be explained explicitly, i.e. what it is for, possible reaction, hoped for outcome, etc. One guy said to me, 'We don't need this, these explanations, not here'. I said that I think we do, the process has to be there. The Shipman business has had a profound effect upon the monitoring of the profession. We are exposed to information that in the past would certainly have been restricted. What you didn't know in the past tended not to concern you, but that said, I'm confident for the future.

There are some things I don't like but there have been fantastic improvements. There are new challenges now: the single parent scenario; AIDS; the drugs problem; and there is violent crime. These are major problems and no doubt more will emerge. Cultural changes about eating, diabetes and obesity are going to be horrendous. So, we will cure heart disease for a lot of people but many others will get the disease because they're overweight and under-exercised. I'm not apportioning blame or fault, it's simply the lifestyle we have today. I am horrified when I see what people eat and how they eat it, out on the streets. Meal times were part of the integration of family life, sitting around together, but now the dining room has been rendered obsolete in many households.

Hopefully, we can reach out and influence, for example, smoking in young males. We seem to have got the idea across that smoking makes you less attractive, makes your breath smell, ruins your health and you lack the wind for competitive sport. Unfortunately, we are not winning with young women, so many of whom think it is chic and adult to smoke. Perhaps we'll end up with the American dichotomy of the very fit on one hand and the obese couch potato on the other.

Another thing I see is the death and regeneration of community and the effect it has on people. In Meltham, we saw the end of David Brown as the American firm Case bought it simply as a franchise to put out of business and so the place virtually died. Now we have a village regenerated and it's vibrant. Marsden was the last of the insular, self-contained villages of the old type that I remember so well. My wife is from Marsden so I have some acceptance in the place. It certainly has some wonderful traditions – the 'Avalanche Dodgers', a group of men who founded a club in order to avoid their wives. Their leader was the local poet Armitage's dad. They put on yearly shows that are well attended and very professional. Marsden also has the 'Cuckoo Festival' and the restored canal system, but, unfortunately, lots of drugs. Yet it remains in some ways a sort of closed community. Mind, it was like that throughout the Holme Valley as well. If you went from Brockholes to Thurstonland, they'd think you'd only come up for a fight. God forbid you should go to Scholes from Brockholes if they'd lost a cricket match. I remember somebody once throwing a half-brick at me outside The Boot & Shoe when I was having a drink. Oh yes, very tribal!

As for retirement, the thought of being divested of my roots is absolutely horrific, it would be like a prison sentence. Sure, I'd go away during drizzly November and March for a holiday but to leave this whole matrix and network that has made up my really rich life would to me be death.

Vera Waddington

painter and a ninety-five year-old Grande Dame of the Holme Valley

I was born in Netherthong in 1911 and lived there until 1922. I have lived in Honley since 1922, a lovely little village with many of the same shops in the centre of the village. Where the bakery is now was a bakery then. The main shops were Drake's store and the Co-op. The Co-op was different in those days; it had a drapery shop, a grocery and greengrocery shop, a butcher and a cobbler. Drake's sold high-class groceries and I remember Moorhouse's and their vans; they had lorries then as they still have. I have recently painted one of Moorhouse's vans coming up Towngate. It will go on sale, I hope, to support sufferers of cystic fibrosis and leukaemia. It's in the pipeline.

I started work as an apprentice mender with another person from Honley, Olive Brown, as she is now, and who now lives in Berry Brow. We're not able to meet these days but we are good friends. I worked for a clothier's shop for a bit down King Street in Huddersfield while I was waiting for the apprenticeship. We had to go on the No.10 tram from the bottom of Towngate. We started work at 9.00 a.m. and finished at 7.00 p.m. but on Friday it was 8.00 p.m. and on Saturday 9.00 p.m. That was the working week as a shop assistant. Then I was so fortunate to become an apprentice, I could now play tennis on Saturday. The apprenticeship was here in Honley, at Josiah France's which has long gone. Huddersfield was, of course, a textile town in the 1920s and most of its people worked in the mills.

I used to think the valley was better when we had an Urban District Council; then you were with your own people. I do think it was better than its replacement, Kirklees, but I'm old and you've got to move with the times. The council offices were where the offices near the bridge are now. I've a dictionary I got when the council introduced gas ovens into Honley. They had a demonstration down there and we children at the local schools were asked if we would mix a loaf of bread and put it in one of the ovens. I won the dictionary for the best loaf and I've still got the dictionary. I've lived in this house for eighty-three years, since 1922, and I never want to leave it.

I started painting when I went to work in town. I was near the Tech so I enrolled for still life at art classes. I won prizes for drawing antique details and this was with the day students, this really lifted me. An MP called Greenwood came to present the prizes. I remember him shaking hands with me and saying, 'Stick to it'. I was longing to be a day student but I had to go to work in the mill. It was a luxury to be an art student in those days and I couldn't afford to be.

I always had a love for painting, even when I was at Honley School. I remember a Turner on the wall, I can see it now, 'The light of the world'. You see, it was painting that enthralled me, I wasn't much good at arithmetic. I've produced hundreds of paintings and I've a book with the details

HONLEY

URBAN DISTRICT COUNCIL.

Presented to

VERA KENYON

as an Award and Token

of Appreciation

of

A GOOD LOAF OF BREAD

BAKED IN A GAS OVEN.

Dec. 13th, 1923.

12 YEARS OLD.

Vera's award for a good loaf of bread, 1923. (V. Waddington)

Watercolour print. (V. Waddington)

Watercolour print. (V. Waddington)

Vera in December 2006.

of every one of them written down. It's very much a hobby, even more so since becoming a widow. My daughter Christine said, 'Mum…paint!', and I have, ever since. I know where all the main ones are. I think the best was of a bridge in the Clwyd Valley in Wales. Rural scenes and flowers are my favourite subjects. Perhaps my personal favourite is of a clematis which was on that wall you can see through the window. It's gone now. My living room is my studio, though that may sound strange.

I liked working for Holmfirth Art Week and Huddersfield Art Society. I was made a lifetime member, at ninety-three, but having no transport of my own, I have been reliant on friends with cars. We'd go out for the day. I used to paint at the site but in recent years I take photographs and colour notes and then work at home. I think now that I must have painted most of the Holme Valley over the years, though these days there are many of us painting. I've never been commercial though I have painted some postcard scenes for a kitchen manufacturer.

You know, I do remember Armistice Day in 1918. I was seven and all the young children linked arms and sang 'Keep the home fires burning'. My uncle had been a POW and he came back so changed. It had been a very bitter experience as a prisoner of war. When I was eleven I remember at Christmas we took the turkey up to my grandmother's house in Deansbrook. It was so big we had to wheel it up in a pram. What days.

George Slater

sometime president of the Huddersfield Choral Society

I was actually born in Paris, France not Hepworth, though my parents were Yorkshire people. My father gained a scholarship to study in Paris; thereafter he got a job and became a cloth agent, running his own business from Paris until 1930, when I was born. He contracted disseminated sclerosis and we came back to Huddersfield. I had only spent six months in France, far too young and definitely not long enough to acquire the language.

I eventually joined the family clothing manufacturing business, H. Booth & Son Ltd, founded by my grandfather Henry in 1903. Originally located in St John's Road, later moving to John William Street in Huddersfield, it was burned down in a disastrous fire in 1942. Because of labour restrictions production had to be moved to a 'distressed area'. The nearest of these was twenty-five miles away in Hoyland Common, near Barnsley, where the only major employment available was in mining. There was nothing for women to do, at least before the war, but to go into service. So, there was a large untapped female labour force which proved to be extremely hard working, loyal and, after training, skilful.

I joined the Choral, singing bass on 2 April 1954. I have received a silver salver to mark my 50th anniversary and I am now one of the seven Hon. Life members. The Choral was founded in 1836 and we had our 150th anniversary on 6 June 1986. I had enjoyed the presidency from 1982-84. As president one is the figurehead for the society and there is a clear administrative role.

The connection between Methodism and the Choral was traditionally strong but that training ground for singers is largely gone now as the church has declined. University music has in a way replaced our Methodist chapels as a supplier of talent. The strength of the choir is now about 200, with the ranges all well represented. We are not short of tenors, unlike some, thanks to a good recruitment campaign. We currently have people from Lancashire, from Silsden, Leeds, Bradford in West Yorkshire, from Northallerton in North Yorkshire and from Sheffield in the South. At one time, particularly when the church was strong, the choir was, of course, much more parochial.

It all started when sixteen like-minded people came together in 'The Plough Inn' in Westgate to form the society. The Preamble, as it was called, declared: 'We whose names are hereunto subscribed agreed to Establish a Musical Society to be called the 'Huddersfield Choral Society', the first Meeting to be held in the Infant School Room, Spring Street, on Friday the 15th day of July 1836 at Eight o'clock in the Evening; the succeeding Meetings to be held on the Friday on or before the full moon, in every month.' Given that this was

George and Nancy Slater at the 2006 *Messiah*, Huddersfield Town Hall.

130 years ago the names of the sixteen are almost all unsurprisingly associated with the Huddersfield area.

Any of the ladies, if they had 'singing status', either as amateurs or professionals, were known as 'madams' – Madam Emily Harrop, Madam Muriel McKean, for example. Indeed, to become a madam was real achievement, it was an envied status. Most ladies wore hats at the AGM. It was a very decorous and formal occasion in those days.

The current concert ensemble is the dinner jacket for men and the ladies in French blue. As always we have more women than men. The ideal ratio is four sopranos to three altos and one tenor to two bass. The possibility of a lady presidency was a novel innovation. I recall talking to a couple of ladies in the bar after a concert during Arwel Hughes' tenure. They were wondering how a lady might get to become an officer. I suggested that there was no reason why they shouldn't become officers and in the event Sandy Cole became the first lady president and we have one at the moment, Margaret Atkinson. The committee is about seventeen to eighteen, ladies to gentlemen, so very well represented, but it was getting through to the upper echelon in the past that was difficult. Now we're completely democratic.

The future is certainly optimistic, though like all such organizations we have had our peaks and troughs. Sir Malcolm Sargent was resident conductor from 1933 until the time of his death in 1967. He was the guiding light and he arranged what we would sing, the soloists and the orchestra. I was certainly in awe of him, a great figure, and I sang under Sir Malcolm for thirteen years.

George at the Barbican; coming off stage after Puccini's Turandot, 1982. (G. Slater)

Huddersfield Choral, *Messiah*, 2002. (G. Slater)

We've only had eleven conductors in 169 years: he was there for thirty-four of them, a long tenure. He originated from Stamford, in Lincolnshire and came up through church music to London where he became known as 'Flash Harry'. His residency was a peak period for us and after his death we sort of drifted for a while, doing our own thing, having lost such a great character.

Sir William Walton wrote for us and in 1961 he composed the *Gloria*. He was very late in finishing this work, we were practising and we still hadn't got it all together. In the end the performance was a bit ropey and I remember Walton coming down the aisle of the town hall during a rehearsal while Sir Malcolm was on the podium. Walton announced, 'This isn't good enough!' 'Well come up and conduct it yourself', retorted Sargent, the heat of the moment and two powerful characters colliding.

Martin Brabbins is our current conductor; he's been with us for about four years. Jane Glover, our previous conductor-in-chief, is now principal guest conductor; she and Martin share it between them. She was resident for six years. The town hall is our secret weapon given the wonderful acoustics but the audience has, unfortunately, to be uncomfortable and there can only be 1,200 of them. So, performances tend to be special.

We have travelled all over: Vienna, Brussels, Munich, Oporto, Lisbon, Berlin with the Berlin Philharmonic, Boston, Bratislava and Brno. I would love to go back to the Musikverein in Vienna – a peak musical memory. We had such a wonderful reception in 1958 with Sir Malcolm to do the *Messiah*, *Belshazzar's Feast* and Faure's *Requiem*. The reception for the performance of the *Messiah* went on for twenty minutes. They were standing, applauding and cheering. I have never seen or heard any thing like it before or since. Strangely enough, they're not used to hearing the *Messiah* on the Continent. Sir Malcolm had in fact to teach the Vienna Symphony how to play it. There was an afternoon rehearsal before an evening concert. So, he had to lick them into shape without the benefit of language but in the end the performance was stupendous – to think that Handel composed the thing in three weeks. My favourite soloist with the *Messiah* was Marjorie Thomas, the alto. She sang with the choir and Sir Malcolm for many years and we had a very special relationship with her, and indeed, of course, with the old ones from the recordings: Elsie Morrison, soprano, Gladys Ripley, alto, Norman Walker, the bass and the tenor, James Johnstone.

Mike Hirst

flute player and Huddersfield Old Boy … wherever he is

Professionally, a lot of my colleagues who provided me with work from 1970 have now passed on or have retired. A new generation occupies the top seats of the London orchestras, for the most part. I've not totally retired but the sort of dates I do now are minimal. The last enterprise I did was a wedding do for cash at Dulwich College. The groom was the lad who looked after our motors. At the opening we primarily played Mozart's *Flute Quartets*, to 'keep the old tone high'.

I played with the five main orchestras, the LSO, LPO, the Philharmonia, the Royal Philharmonic and the BBC Symphony, at various times as a freelance player. As a player you must be able to get on with all the section. I was with many freelance groups, West End shows, BBC schools' music and lots of tours around Europe and the US. The first flute is always the person who tells the 'fixer' who to book. He may not be the very best player but he's the player who knows what's what. He's welcome wherever, knows who's who. You know, 'we don't want that bloke again'. The second flute at the LSO told me, 'We've decided you're not as good as we thought you were going to be'. He wanted to put my back up.

As a freelance in later life, the early 1990s, I was guest principal flute for the English String Orchestra which expanded to take in the rest. Yehudi Menuhin, lovely chap, was hired as guest conductor. I remember I had to drive him from Worcester to Bath one awful night in driving rain. I thought, 'if we skid off the road and crash I will be forever known as the man who killed Yehudi Menuhin'. He was asleep for most of the journey.

In the 1970s I was with the English Drawing Room, two or three singers, cello and flute. As well as playing we dressed up in period gear for eighteenth century Georgian and nineteenth century Victorian, then did foppish acting and reading. One critic dismissed my reading as appalling. We did a Georgian concert at a stately home in Gloucestershire. Fires were lit in normally unlit fireplaces, smoke rolled in while we trying to sing and play. One of the singers, Linda Hirst, from Beaumont Park in Huddersfield (no relation), lent me her jumper which I had to wear inverted as period pantaloons, not having the appropriate keks with me.

A big thing about London orchestras when they went on tour was that they became different people. A particular European tour nearly had the entire orchestra chucked off the plane. The captain said we were the worst lot they'd ever transported, worse than any football crowd they'd moved. A member of the orchestra, the worse for wear, confronted a contemporary composer who was present and while accounting him a decent-enough fellow told him his music was a load of crap – all good-natured banter.

String players, in particular, can be very

Mike and flute. (M. Hirst)

welcome in one orchestra but poison in another. Nobody ever says anything, of course, it's just shunting people around, another bloke in your chair. I did have the distinction of being with the Birmingham Symphony for about five and a half years and then with the Bournemouth. Before Birmingham I was living here in Huddersfield, at Newsome where I was born and bred.

When I was in Huddersfield, my roots, the first job I had was delivering newspapers at thirteen. My father was a grocer, as Alan Bennett's father was a butcher in Leeds, similar background. My mother had to leave school at fourteen to work in the mill. Don't know how she met my father, didn't get to hear about that. They had to struggle to find enough money to put down for the mortgage for the house on Lockwood Scar, which I still have. They managed and that's where I grew up. I went to Mount Pleasant School in Lockwood. It was fairly ordinary, I went in at the age of five and came out the other end at fifteen. I mean, even at school we weren't expected to be academic. We were supposed to be plasterers, mill workers, labourers, etc. Mother and the rest used to discuss who I'd got it from when I started with the flute.

I could read and write but little else except play the flute, which I learned from my Lockwood music mistress, having played the triangle in the percussion band. She must have seen some future talent in me, 'Michael, would you like to learn the flute?' They had an old one there and after that I couldn't put the thing down. I was eleven and carried on, I think, because everybody in our class failed to go to grammar school. Music had just been introduced into the education service at that time.

I was born in January 1939. Mother was very worried because she thought the Germans would come along and chuck us

With the English Drawing Room, 1970s. (M. Hirst)

Llandudno, 1958. (M. Hirst)

all into the street. Apparently she ran out in a panic and hared off down the road with me in her arms when war was declared. She was a very nervous woman, German paratroopers everywhere. Of course, like Leeds we weren't really bombed at all.

I was so keen to do the flute and somehow make a career of it but the only people I knew who made money out of music were the peripatetic teachers who filled in by playing for the local amateurs and getting musicians' union rates. As I grew up I played for a lot of the local amateur operatic societies. I got £3-4 a week and got around on the bus. I thought, 'how can I keep on playing the flute?' My mother's brothers and sisters were saying, 'What's lad gah'n to do?' 'Well, he wants to play the flute'. 'Oh bloody 'ell. Get 'im in t'mill'. But one uncle said no, it's a good wheeze. He'd been in the navy and said, 'You want to get 'im in an Army or Navy band, you get payed for playin' and you'd be doin' next to nothin'. Well, I thought this might be a good idea so I wrote to some Army place in York to be a band boy, or something, because people a few years older than me were doing National Service and a couple had got into the Coldstream Guards' band in London. Without realizing what the Army would be really like, I thought this might be the thing.

My mother, though, had a mighty shock when she heard about this, with my father only recently dead. She felt incredibly lonely and she was motivated to go shooting down to the music department at the Tech, where the university is now, and talk to Mr Williams who knew me very well. She said, 'Our Michael, you know, wants to go into the music profession, but we don't know'. 'Well Mrs Hirst, we'll start him on O and A levels. He's got to get a qualification'. So, on those terms and a little bursary from being assistant librarian for the Tech, gramophone 78s and other stuff, I carried on playing the flute. I managed A level Music (just) and History, as well as some O levels. These enabled me to go to St Mark and St John C of E Teacher Training College in Chelsea for two years. The college has since repaired to Plymouth. I also managed to miss National Service.

Before that, I have to tell you, I joined the musicians' union ASAP when I was about seventeen or eighteen, so that I could earn better fees with the local operatics. Such was the competition that I got in on this lark – doing 'White Horse Inn', 'Call me Madam' and really 'interesting stuff' like that, and very grateful for it indeed. The power of the union was great. Unknown to me, the chap who led the orchestra for the Huddersfield Amateurs was a Bradford man called John Atkinson, who had a concert name of John Morava because he'd spent some time in Moravia. He was also in charge of the music on Llandudno Pier. In 1958 I was going to do a few more O levels but I got a call from this bloke asking me to come and play from June through to September as his flute player had gone elsewhere.

We were in digs in Llandudno, bacon and eggs at 9.00 a.m., then walk from the digs to the pier for the morning concert, starting at 11.00 a.m. Played some rubbish then had coffee in the pavilion café. Then we played the second half, finishing about 12.20 and then back to the digs for meat, two veg and roly poly pud. Might sleep in the afternoon then the gong would go for pork pies, salad and cakes. I grew enormously. This was a seven-day-a-week job playing reasonably popular light music. There was another Huddersfield chap playing there, Tony Moran, who died recently. His brother had The Albert in town and, unusually, Tony was the only musician in a big Irish family. In Llandudno we stuck together a bit even

Above and left: Mellors Groceries (Tinker and Hurst), King Street, 1935. (M. Hirst)

Mike's parents (left) at Morecambe, August 1935. (M. Hirst)

though he was thirteen years older. We used to go to The Clarence for a beverage and then roll back to the digs to find that our landlady had left sandwiches out for us – a little midnight snack. Mother came to Llandudno with Aunt Annie for a week. Auntie Hilda had to write, you know, to tell them who'd died, who'd been in hospital for operations, had to keep up with the news.

I went to the library in Llandudno and found a book on health foods. I thought I've got to stop eating as my clothes were beginning to stretch. I cancelled the bacon and eggs in favour of brown bread and honey, and a lot of good it did me, I had a heart attack when I was sixty-four. They stick a sort of Channel Tunnel-type scraper through your arteries until they find the blockage and then poke it out.

Anyway, while I was doing the training college stint for two years, I claimed back the tax from salaries I'd earned. I would get a job teaching in 1960/1, working part time at a big comp at Forest Hill in London. It was run like a public school with traditional houses. I'd had to get the train from Llandudno to Euston, leaving most of my clothes on the train. The college had accommodation in the first year; after that, I bicycled in from Fulham. Then I met other musicians and got lessons from the best teacher of the day, Geoffrey Gilbert. He normally taught only those who were at the music college in London. I could have gone to the RCM, I had a free entrance but no money. So, I was fortunate. I did my brief teaching stint but then my Aunt Annie said, ''Ah think y'ought to come back t'uddersfield. Your mother's missin' you a lot'. She shamed me into returning.

Mike and mum at Llandudno. (M. Hirst)

My earliest tour abroad was when I was fifteen. We went to Germany in a spirit of reconciliation and we were seen off in great style from Huddersfield. Loads of folk turned out to wave bon voyage. In Germany we were given a tour of the VW factory and at this tender age I first witnessed what might be called bad behaviour among members of orchestras, on tour.

I got a job at the Leeds Grand: they ran a little orchestra, about ten players. As long as the theatre was open, even if you weren't required to play, you got a £10 retainer. That was 1962/3, and when Sadlers Wells or the Royal Opera came I just breezed in, sat in the best seats and enjoyed it. The worst thing was the panto, which went on and on. I had to play the sax as well, self taught of course. The comedians used to make jokes about my totally hopeless playing. I just blew into it and sold it as soon as possible.

I still carried on at Llandudno summer season from 1958 till 1963 when I saw a *Guardian* ad in the library for the Birmingham Symphony Orchestra for third flute to double with piccolo. I applied and was interviewed. John gave me the morning off and I got back in time for the evening concert. He was very good with helping people to better themselves. I was offered the job on the spot, though nobody knew or had heard of me, just heard me play. The conductor said, 'We'd like you to join the orchestra, would £25 per week be satisfactory?' An enormous amount: we were on about fifteen quid on the pier. The married ones were paying £4 10s for their digs and sending the rest home.

I never felt the need for money in my whole life, even though my mother thought we were going to starve. The sum I was being paid was a principal's fee. When my wife to be, a violinist, joined, she got about £15. We stayed there until 1968. I came up to Huddersfield while my mother was enduring Alzheimer's, before she went into Storthes Hall, which they were even then considering closing. I would sometimes do a concert while I was up there. So, I kept contact with people in Huddersfield and when my mother eventually died in 1990 I thought it would be stupid to sell the place. I went to the Poly, as it then was, seeking a suitable person to live in a non-smoking private house not designed for student accommodation. They found just the right bloke who's been there ever since.

I still feel affection for Huddersfield after London. My wife's doubtful: she thinks I'm more keen on Huddersfield than I am on her. Well, there are no arguments and you can always talk on the phone. Of course, the place has shot up in value though I've done nothing to it. My parents paid about £300 for it in 1937.

My wife and myself went to see a play called *Huddersfield*, written by a Siberian writer – strong language and ooh, lots of simulated eroticism. It received four stars in the *Guardian* review. Basically, it alluded to *Hamlet*. The young girl in the play comes for lessons as Hamlet but what she gets instead are lessons on sex from an alcoholic, relentlessly smoking Russian. It was about the fiasco that's occurred since the end of Communism when many people found themselves to be much worse off. The writer actually came to Huddersfield to put on a play at the Lawrence Batley Theatre. The language mustn't have been so strong, and he had memories of the rain and how boring the place was. So that's the connection, according to him.

I haven't told you about my great aunt who lived in Lockwood. The only thing I really enjoyed when growing up there was music and the cinema, 'Lockwood Pictures', now

Mike, Tony Moran, Jack McCormack and Barry Castle, with Peggy Castle in Tucson. (M. Hirst)

Great-aunt Nelly and great-uncle Johnny. (M. Hirst)

Mike in 2006.

an engineering place. My aunt lived close to the traffic lights. From her place you just turned left towards town and there was a little place that had concerts near the Lockwood and Salford Con Club before you got to the cinema. At the pictures they changed the film every Thursday night, two a week, and you got an A and a B film. My great aunt, who brought up my father because they didn't have enough room in his house, hadn't read one book in her life but on Mondays she always went to the pictures and I went with her, whatever they were showing.

She had a great profession, which has gone out of use now. She didn't have qualifications and she worked for the local undertaker, Arnold Quarmby. He had a joinery place that was started in the 1850s – joinery, funerals, the lot. The place is still there but I don't know if it is inhabited. Arnold, in his nineties, was still living a couple of years ago.

In the 1940s, when a person died, if they hadn't been carted off to the infirmary the body would be sent to the undertaker and my auntie went along to lay them out. One day, for whatever reason, she took me along to see her handiwork. The body was in one of those high buildings at Lockwood crossroads that were built in the 1830s for tourists who'd come for the Baths in Albert Street, to take the waters. So, these accommodations were rented out to summer visitors. Well, we climbed up lots of stairs and went into a musky room with the curtains closed. I vaguely saw this dead body on top of the bed. I must have been about five or six and later that night I didn't seem to be able to get off to sleep. Next day, my mother went down and gave her a terrible b★★★★★★ing. Great aunt was the central figure in Lockwood; when she went away in the ambulance, something usually presaging doom, she was waving goodbye to everybody and telling them all she'd be back, and she was. She lived till almost eighty-nine, which was very good going for ordinary folk in those days.

Stuart Coldwell

fell walker and ex-mill owner

The Masters' Hike

The Masters' Hike ran from Salendine Nook, over Pole Moor, up to Holme Moss and on to Emley. Initially it was for Scouts, then any youth organizations, now your fell runners, a funny lot, want to run all the way round – twenty-six miles, it was certainly challenging. This story concerned a fellow, we'll call him Bob, a strange one, spent too much time talking to sheep. He was a gamekeeper in the fastnesses up on the tops. At one time he lived in an old lodge right out on the moor, no mains at all, and he was chums with a similar character who lived close by. You don't actually meet these people, you just see them wandering out on the moor.

One of the big checkpoints on the hike was near a main road junction. These two characters were on Water Board land, though they acted as though they owned it. There was a big marquee set up for the rescue team. Anyone who hadn't made it from Salendine Nook to the check point by 4.00 p.m. was to be stopped, and then the rescue team would sweep through to pick up any one who'd been missed. Anyway, Bob came down larging it about not having given his permission for us to put up the tent. He got a shotgun out of his car and made menacing gestures towards the tyres off the organizers' cars. The lad who was the inspiration behind the hike had with him in his briefcase the previous year's letter of acknowledgement. Covering the date up with his finger, he showed it to Bob. 'Bloody 'ell', he said, 'I must've been asleep that day'. Aye!

The hike, quite a bit of it, was on undefined paths, not easy walking. They used to limit it to 125 teams of four. Last time I heard any news they were struggling to raise fifty teams. When I was involved in the thing, it was heavily oversubscribed. On the stretch from Holme Moss to Saltersbrook there was no open access at all; there was a public footpath on the Derbyshire side which wasn't where the hike wanted to go and they wouldn't allow anyone to just walk, the Water Board insisted on the tenants giving their permission. People working in harsh conditions the year round didn't make for sociability.

Scouting

I was never in Scouting as a lad but I eventually did twelve years with the local Scout troop, six of those with the District Scout Fellowship. Some of the lads in that were more regional than I was and their annual 'big effort' was the Masters' Hike. Our friend Bob found a plastic bag up on the moor a week after the hike. He rang up one of the lads with a demand that someone go up 'now' and pick it up. A lad went up to get it and it turned out to be a fertilizer bag from one of the farms up there. Bob was decidedly unpleasant.

A more amusing story of hill farmers took place above Scammonden. In this particular place there were two sisters and a brother, all in their seventies. One sister had never left the farm and the other had left it once or twice. He left the place a couple of times a year for flour and salt, otherwise they were self sufficient – if you can imagine being self sufficient up there. One day he said to the lad delivering the mail, 'What's it like down in town now, lad?' 'Oh, they've built a nice new ring road, a sports centre and a big new indoor market'. 'By heck', he said, 'I never thought Slathwaite'd 'ave owt like that.'

Great-grandmother

She died about 1930 and in her will her estate was to be divided between her three sons. One of them had been killed at the Somme in 1916. So, we're in 1930 now, picture her frame of mind. My father is named after Hubert who was lost in the First World War. In 1930 she left about £6,000, a great deal of money at that time. My great-grandfather never worked out how she'd done it. Seems she used to invest her shillings, two bobs and half crowns in the stock market. The money was divided between my grandfather and his brother. In truth, it was like a lottery in 1930. So, the brother stopped working immediately, took up doing all sorts that didn't involve work, whatever he wanted. Apparently his wife never washed any clothes: she went out and bought new ones. In the early 1930s my dad went with him to Barnsley to collect a new car. They went by bus and drove the new vehicle back. When they got back dad said the car wasn't pulling very well, then discovered they'd driven all the way with the handbrake on.

Well, my grandfather bought the site at Cocking Mill, formerly John Wrigley's. He had looked at another site, I believe, at the bottom of Station Street in Meltham; there was an old cotton mill there, where Morrisons is now. Wrigley's were livery-cloth manufacturers and they'd gone out of business about 1923-4. I've no idea what he paid for it although I've got all the legal documents. I must look through. When you closed your business for good you were obliged to keep all your records for six years afterwards. So, I suppose I'll be shredding old invoices, wage books and the rest. The older documents I've kept on one side. They're on vellum and go right back to 1812. It's all hand written and my aim is to transcribe and type them. There's no punctuation with these things as it affected meaning, so they avoided it. There was a mill on the site in 1720 and the documents I have actually refer to that date. The buildings there in my time were mid-nineteenth century in origin. The earliest was from 1830 and it's now converted into flats. There's not an awful lot of documentation from 1812, perhaps three or four, then they go on to the 1920s when Wrigley's shut down and the ownership changed.

The Wrigleys lived off Lea Lane, at Field House. We had a visit from one a few years ago: he wanted to find out where the family home had been. They had actually decamped to somewhere in the North Riding. The trade they were in, livery cloth, had been there for hundreds of years, yet within the space of forty years the whole thing disappeared completely. The fabric they made was what the driver of a coach and four would wrap around himself, a heavy-felted, heavily-milled, solid fabric which, by virtue of its weight and lanolin treatment, was waterproof. That affected a lot of the textile industry in the area – overtaken by history.

Above and below: Sections of the Wrigley Indenture.

Stuart, 2006.

With such a specialization, you couldn't suddenly decide to do something else, you weren't set up for it.

There were a lot of strange goings-on up and down the valley. There's the tale about Joseph Sykes' at Brockholes. The young girls there had quite a reputation. When a young lad started there as an apprentice the lasses used to trap him under the wicker skips and do nasty things to 'im. In the early 1960s they used to bus girls in from Barnsley – the nickname they had is now unrepeatable. They'd have your keks off and slap machine grease over you if you weren't careful. What a crowd, we used to see them on the bus and one or two'd think nothing of the lewdest gestures.

In Huddersfield, the worsted industry has contracted in the same way as the woollen industry. One group, Huddersfield Fine Worsteds, had advertisements in the trade magazine, *The Wool Record*. They would advertise all these lovely old names such as Josiah France, Learoyds, etc. None of these places was actually still in existence. They were just names from the past taken up by one company. The family of James Mason, Huddersfield's most famous Hollywood star, were big shareholders in Illingworth Morris whose main centre was in Saltaire. Mason, I think, was a Fixby lad, somewhere up there.

Huddersfield was fortunate in the 1960s in one respect in that as the worsted and woollen sectors contracted there was expansion in the chemical and light engineering industries. Now, they've gone into decline. We look to be going into the 'Big Mac' culture, the so-called service sector. Manufacturing's gone to the wall; you can't have an economy based on the service sector, you have to be making something. If everybody's working in the service business, then there's no money. It pays so badly the local economy will grind to a halt. You can't bring up a family on the wages paid in the service sector. The textile industry in my time was relatively low paid but certainly enough to raise a family: there was overtime and you could afford to buy a home with it. You need a fortune to buy a house of any kind today.

If you look at the shops in Huddersfield, virtually all the middle to the better end of the trade's gone anyway. There's just one small gents' outfitters on Cloth Hall Street, Beatties has a men's section, after that it's M&S: high-class outfitting's gone. You've to go to Leeds or Manchester for that.

Back on the tops

My brother was surveying up there when they were building the M62 and he said there was real animosity between the locals and the contractors – very bad feeling. The locals were seeing what they felt would be the end of their way of life and they couldn't do anything about it. On the other side of the coin they were probably well compensated. It was only by chance that the motorway was routed across the dam at Scammonden. The dam builders and motorway people were not from the same authority and the two sets of surveyors saw each other up there – we're building a dam, we're building a motorway. Then the decision was taken to run the road across the dam wall. Where else could they have put it?

We went to some talks by the LA who were trying to sell sailing at Scammonden reservoir. It's a fine stretch of water but it's very definitely high moorland weather. There was a thought that we might abandon sailing at Redbrook and move *en bloc* to Scammonden because of the size of the water; it didn't happen. That club that has survived with some enthusiasm is Huddersfield SC, which sails up at Boshaw Whams: that's even smaller than Redbrook. Local scouting has lost its sailing and canoeing because of the cost of insurance and the stipulation that there must be instruction from a fully-qualified member of a relevant club, membership held for at least three years. Well, that didn't happen either.

Arthur Quarmby

architect; extracts from our conversation

Huddersfield's architecture

Kirklees is in the habit of neglecting many of its old buildings and the town library is a case in point. They much prefer to neglect them than pull down and rebuild. I don't think it's in too bad a state at all: it's newer than the Empire State building in New York and, indeed, many other iconic buildings. It has some delights, it has some failures in its function, of course, but I have no confidence in them being able to put back anything half as good.

The art gallery doesn't work very well and libraries are different places to when this building was conceived. I do like the staircase but the disabled access is very poor; isn't it everywhere? I sing in the town hall with the Huddersfield Choral and the Colne Valley Male Voice Choir and very little attempt has been made to provide for disabled people.

Both of the Co-op buildings are excellent, in my opinion. The 1930s building was wonderful, it had canopies that floated and there was glazing both above and below. They were taken off and replaced with absolute rubbish, horrid, nasty lumpen things. The flagpole was part of the focus of the design and they've put that somewhere else altogether. A case of bad ownership, I'm afraid, but these were two excellent buildings.

Perhaps best of all is the Ramsden Estate Office building, underused of course. I think they just sold off all the Ramsden estate and spent it on Batley and Dewsbury, thus neglecting this wonderful building.

It's a curious thing: you remember the prefabs built after the war? Some of them were kit built by redundant aircraft factories – not like 'proper' houses at all. They had big windows, proper kitchens and bathrooms. They were of concrete or aluminium panel construction and didn't look like houses as we knew them yet the prefab was a small detached home with a garden all the way around. You can drive round the country and see many still in use. You consider the tall municipal tower blocks with their life span of about thirty years: they don't last anywhere near as long as the prefabs. There's something that should be learned from that.

Family

I was born in Huddersfield and my family was certainly here as long ago as 1150. The first one that I know of was Adam FitzOrm, obviously upwardly mobile to use the prefix 'Fitz' rather than the suffix 'son'. He didn't adopt all the Norman traits – they were in the habit of leaving everything to the eldest son. He left the Kirkheaton estate to his eldest and the Quarmby estate to his second, which is why our coat of arms has a little martlet on the top to indicate a second son. Loads of gaps after that, of course, and

Arthur fronting some of the town's best. (*Huddersfield Examiner*)

apart from the bloody feud in the 1300s our family have lived here with no particular distinction at all. Is that some sort of record? You'd think they'd have done summat in all that time.

There was no tradition of architecture in the family. I come from five generations of butchers. My mother was taken out of school at thirteen and stuck in the mill as a weaver: she absolutely hated it. She was determined that her children were going to have a decent education. My father had gone to Almondbury Grammar School and how she persuaded him I don't know but instead of going there they sent me to Pocklington in the East Riding. This was quite an eye-opener: I was an average treble hereabouts but quite a star in the East Riding. Music became a large part of my life at the school as the facilities were there for it. My teacher was the organist and choir-master at Beverley Minster – Johnny Long with his 18hp red sports car and his spotted bow tie.

My father thought I was spending too much time on music. I wasn't spending any time on sport because I was only eight stone. When we were playing rugby my friends used to pick me up and run off with me. Father cut off all my music lessons but the school gave me a little scholar-ship to continue them. I wanted to be in music but my father said, 'There's no brass in it lad. You'd better be an auctioneer or an accountant'. He was working his way through the alphabet and as I could draw a bit he stopped at architect.

Earth-sheltered structures

My house was designed to be fun to live in rather than being energy efficient but it is both. We've been here thirty years and it's still fun. It was the first of its kind to be built in Britain, apart from the ancient ones, of course.

In 1943 the Luftwaffe finally got the Rolls Royce aero-engine factory in Coventry, where they made the V12 Merlin. So, in eight months, a quarter of a million square feet of factory production was carved out of the soft red sandstone inside Kinver Edge. When I heard that BMW, who now own RR, were planning to build an earth-sheltered production space for RR cars I wrote to them saying that there was no need to do that as one already existed. They were only intending to have a structure with a grass roof of course. Curiously enough, over the Drakelow Depot, as it was called, there were ancient rock-cut houses.

Around here we have sandstone as well as millstone grit, which isn't the fine sandstone you'll get off Crosland Moor. As it weathers the 'fines' are washed off and it's left looking very rough and coarse. Gritstone has been used for ashlar: look at old local houses with mullioned windows, they look very rough now.

Building types other than houses are much more suitable for losing into the ground, visitor centres particularly. I've designed several yet not one has been built properly. Take Rheged up in Cumberland: there the client came to me with a planning refusal. He wished to build a visitor centre

Reconstruction of Mount Pleasant School, 1985. (A. Quarmby)

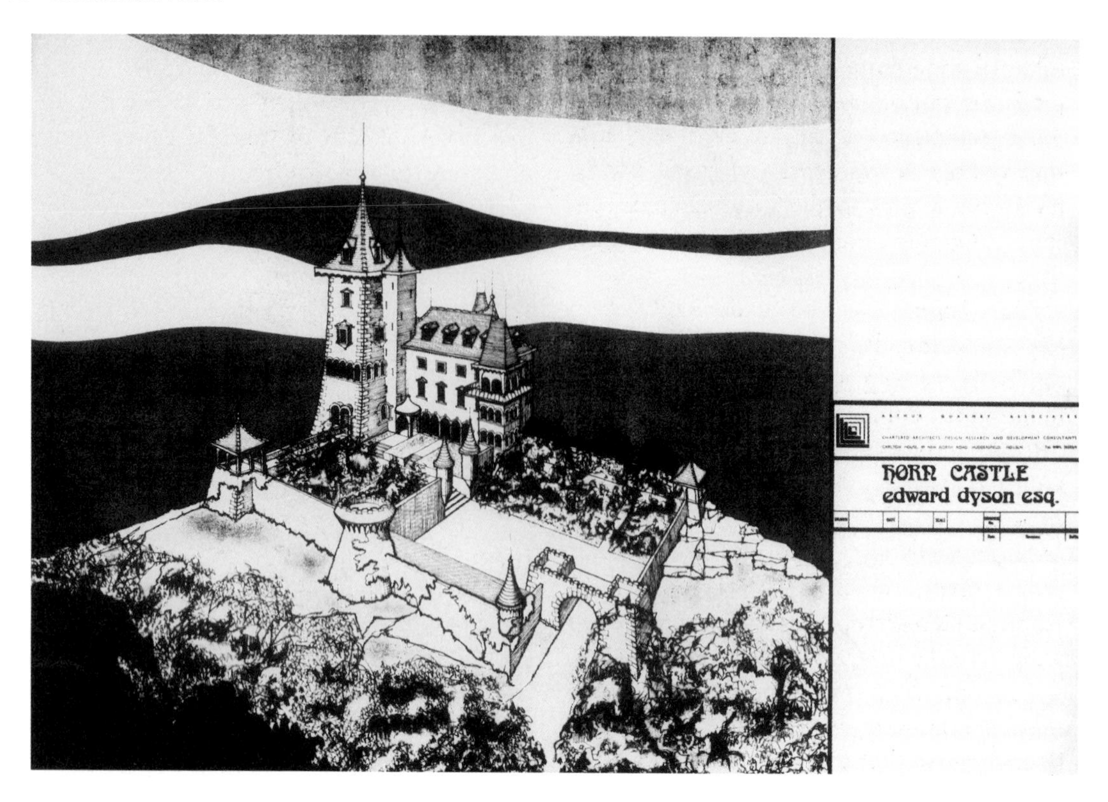

Above and left: The design for Horn Castle, 1973, and its proposed setting above New Mill. (A. Quarmby)

to serve the whole of the Lake District, to catch the visitors as they came off the M6. So, I redesigned it in an earth-sheltered way and it was approved, easy as pie, but he then gave it back to the original architects. It's a shopping centre now, no more than that.

The Bronte Museum decided upon expansion: they hated the extension around the back of the parsonage so I redesigned it into that sloping field that comes down behind. That was approved but they then said that they didn't fancy working underground. I tried to get them to come here to show them that it's not what you think but it died a death. They couldn't agree amongst themselves, I think they enjoyed the scrap.

I'm still moderately busy with earth-sheltered houses, from Spain to Hardraw, to Youlgreave. I did the world's first motor auction in the round in Tucson. Interesting the way car dealers speak to you. 'Trust me mate, this car's perfect'. 'I don't, I'm not your mate and it isn't'.

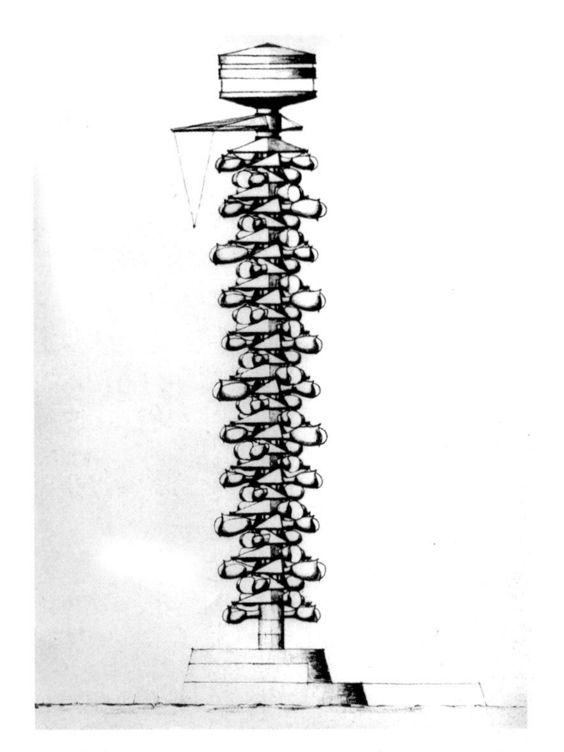

'Corn on the Cob', a 1960s multi-storey living project. (A. Quarmby)

The Holme Graveship

The title I have is, as far as I can make out, of the oldest elected office in the country. When the Normans came over here they had a lot more wit than Blair and Bush in Iraq because they inherited an already established 'feudal' system, only replacing the top layer with their own people. The rent collector they installed in this part of the world was the Grave or Graf. The Manor of Wakefield, still the biggest in England, was a royal manor from the time of Edward the Confessor. William owned it, of course, as did Richard I and various others. It was divided into twelve graveships or administrative areas, of which Holme was one.

The graveships were policed in a very sensible way: we could do with returning to this. The Holme graveship was made up of seven townships: Holme itself, Austonley, Upperthong, Cartworth, Hepworth, Fulstone and Wooldale. Each of these had a local constable. The townships came together to elect a chief constable who in turn would appoint the seven constables. So, the people of the townships came together to vote for the man they wanted and it was an honorary position. As it took up so much time the appointment was only for a year. Incumbents were glad to get shot of it, it was a nuisance.

I've searched through the records of the manor, available from 1274 to the present day. There is not a single case of the lord of the manor refusing to accept or being prepared to dispute the result of the

Structure designed for the British Antartic Survey, assembled in 1962. (A. Quarmby)

election of the chief constable of a particular graveship. So, my office is Chief Constable of the Graveship of Holme. Elected in the proper way, I swore my oath of allegiance to the sovereign and to the lord of the manor, Lady Diana Miller, daughter of the Duke of Leeds – the manor title goes down through both the male and female lines. She lives in Harare, poor thing, and has no interest in Wakefield at all, I'm afraid.

Local government

What we pay in council tax is about a third of what they spend and there's no cap on it. At the turn of the nineteenth and twentieth centuries Holme, like all the other little townships around here, had its own Urban District Council. There were 300 people here and it had electricity long before Holmfirth because there had been a mill on a fall of water upstream from the village. The mill closed down and a local benefactor put a hydroelectric turbine in there, so Holme had electricity at a flat rate. In certain homes in the village you'll see a little window high up and a light in it, i.e. one light would serve two bedrooms.

Home and Family

We built our first home for a couple with a small baby, as we were, but after ten years we were bursting at the seams with two children who were growing up rapidly so we built this place. We have our quarters

The world's largest transparent air-supported dome for a Twentieth Century Fox feature film. (A. Quarmby)

on one side of the house, the children had theirs on the other, guests up in the corner. Within two or three months of moving in here the children both went off to boarding school and now the next generation's coming along.

Moving on, as we must, I once came across a very good old people's home in Huddersfield. It was called 'The Home for Elderly Vegetarians Ltd' and was up Scar Lane, running up from Milnsbridge. I went in there and found a totally different atmosphere from what we think of as a standard retirement home because the residents all owned the place, having bought shares when they moved in. I recall one of the old ladies in there had been introduced to the last Tsar of Russia. The old ladies were actually in charge while the staff was there to look after their needs. I thought, this is how old people's homes should be.

My mother died of gangrene that spread from her toes while her aunt had a leg removed, it was caught in time. Mother was in agony and all they could say was, 'we can't give her any more pain killers because that would endanger her life'. How many people recognise this scenario? My sister fortunately kicked up a hell of a fuss and said, 'You can't leave her to die in agony, give her morphine!' As you know, we recently had a retired doctor pilloried by the establishment for helping a terminally ill friend to die, absolutely stupid.

My wife was a music teacher in secondary modern schools for the most part.

She was very fortunate as she went to Crow Lane Secondary Modern School as a newly qualified music teacher. The headmaster, a big lovely man said, 'Don't let them do any music, set them tests. Let them find out how little they know. After a fortnight they'll be just begging to sing a song.' The school was wonderful and it produced some brilliant boys, including international gymnasts and quite a few people who've had distinguished careers in academia. The government just had to interfere in education, of course, to end a system that worked well. Being successful is about determination. My son and daughter were brought up to think that you can do anything you want to do if you buckle down and stick to it.

Just before I retired I was in line for a European grant, I've had several before but this time they said they wanted evidence of the establishment of my practice, forty years ago, i.e. some sort of bureaucratic confirmation of establishment. In 1960, of course, I just rented a small office in John William Street, stuck up my plate and started in business. It was and should be as easy as that: who needs to ask bureaucrats? I remember my grandfather complaining to the tax man about his bill, 'You call this unearned income, how do you think I got it?

Fenella the tiger

I have a tale to tell you. There was a tiger living in a terraced house in Holmfirth during the Second World War, a full grown Sumatran tiger living up in Cemetery Road. The Overend family had come from South Africa; they were circus people and they brought two very young tiger cubs back with them: one died, Fenella survived. It lived in the long back garden which was fenced in and children from Nab Secondary School used to come and play with her, ride on her back and so forth. She got out from time to time, which rather worried local people because it was the time of the blackout and nobody fancied meeting a tiger on a dark night.

There was the story of soldiers who were billetted in the disused mill at Ribbleden. One of them had gone up for a walk onto the edge at Cartworth and had fallen asleep on Berry Banks. He woke up to find a tiger standing over him – Fenella lived only about 100 yards away. He reckoned he passed out in shock and when he woke again the tiger had gone. He repeated this to his MO who attributed this to a touch too much of the sun but it was quite true that she had been out that afternoon.

I was once coming down from the moors where we still cut peat – those who live in the graveship have retained the right to cut peat despite the Enclosures Act of the 1830s. Anyway, granddad and I had gone up to collect the dried peat, and we had borrowed a white pony and a cart. We loaded up with peat and were coming back down when we met Fenella. The pony, having never seen anything like this in its life before, knew it was a pony's nightmare, so it started bucking and kicking about. My grandfather took off his jacket and put it over the pony's head and led us through. Fenella didn't make a fuss at all. The only misdemeanour she committed was during a funeral procession up Cemetery Road: she reached out and tore a lady's dress. There are pictures of her, absolutely delightful.

These days who would be able to keep a fully grown tiger in a house? Mr Blair would have something to say about that. Fenella died of old age about 1950 after ten years in Holmfirth. She was big, she was affectionate and she never harmed any of the children she played with. The local bookshop keeps hoping that the book that is her story will be republished as many people ask for it. The lady who brought her here was Cassie Overend.

Favoured Music

My pianist best friend reckons Walton's *First Symphony* is the best piece of English music ever written. The Choral Society commissioned *Dona Nobis Pacem* from Vaughan Williams; it is a sort of lament about the Second World War. I believe they haven't sung it since the 1950s, Vaughan Williams is out of fashion you see. I think it's a much, much better piece of music than Britten's *War Requiem*. Since my heart bypass my short-term memory has gone to pot. Strangely enough though, with music I can still remember.

Robin Hood

Did you know the Little John's bow has been 'taken' from Cannon Hall and spirited away to Scotland? His name was John Naylor and he was buried in Hathersage churchyard. The Naylors of Denby Dale have traditionally been very tall men. Robin Hood reputedly shot his last arrow from Kirklees Priory. Where the arrow fell was where he wished to be buried. It's a good story and I've actually measured the distance from the priory to the reputed burial site, about 800 yards. Could anyone shoot that far? It's possible that a bowman might have used arms against legs on a bow with a huge draw weight if accuracy wasn't required.

Jutinder Pal Singh Birdi

Kenyan Sikh, now a Huddersfield civil engineer

Being a Khalsa Sikh

I have taken the instruction ceremony and in that respect I am a Khalsa Sikh but I probably don't live up to all the ideals. I try my best but it's always something you're striving for rather than achieving and it's very difficult to achieve the absolute ideal. Much depends on how you look at the modern world, I think. With every instrument or voice you can do either good or bad. The same applies for religion: if you become either too introverted or too fanatical about religion then you may create consternation. Religion should never be about creating trouble or difficulty – in fact, the opposite. If you look at Christianity, Sikhism, Hinduism, Islam, Judaism and Buddhism, they all try to teach you a moral code of conduct which in turn tries to set out basic ground rules for people to determine their behaviour. Each one is pointing towards the one creator. All religions recognise that the creator is the same for everybody, yet we go around saying that the way in which we address the creator is the right way, therefore the best way.

Religion is a personal thing: what I believe in shouldn't impact upon your beliefs. As long as you hold to your beliefs correctly, then it shouldn't matter what beliefs other people have or choose to follow. The Sikh religion actually came out of oppression. It was founded at a time when there was the almost inevitable form of trouble, that attitude that my religion's better and more appropriate than yours, etc. The Sikh religion takes from Hinduism and Islam and has absorbed all sorts of faiths and influences. The Guru Granth Sahib has many influences in it. When we bow to the Granth Sahib it is not just to a Sikh guru's sayings but also to the teachings of Hindu saints and Muslim fakirs.

The Punjab

I've never been to the homeland of all Sikhs, the Punjab and, of course, most particularly, Amritsar. I've never even been to India. I was born in 1960, in Kenya, at a time when it was still a colonial country. As you will remember, the British used to call it 'Keenya'. Then, when I was about eight, there was a huge exodus of Asians from East Africa. Even though these were pre-Idi Amin days, there was genuine fear that the African governments were going to start kicking out Asian people, mostly to England. I came over with my mother and sister. We settled in Essex for a while, in Romford. I spent three years in school there: meanwhile, my father was still in Kenya. He was working and his job was not under threat. The situation appeared to settle down so he called us back to Kenya. I stayed there until I did my A levels. Going back had been difficult: there was a steep difference in education between here and Kenya. Here, up to the eleven plus we had barely done a bit of challenging maths and the English we studied hadn't really been structured – it seemed to be mostly play. When I went back, the kids there of my age had been studying Geography, History, Religious Education, the three Sciences and Maths to a much higher standard.

I came back to England to take my degree here, at UMIST (University of Manchester, Institute of Science & Technology). I took a civil engineering degree and then got a job with West Yorkshire County Council, as it then was. There were offices in all of the major towns of the county and, as I had friends in Huddersfield, I came here in 1983 and have lived in the town ever since. Apart from Huddersfield, I've worked in Leeds, Wakefield, Halifax and Bradford, and outside the county in Oldham. I reckon that I have long since been adopted as a Huddersfield lad.

I think that there are at least 5-6,000 Sikhs in Huddersfield, certainly many more if we include those born in the town. There are, I think, two principal types of Sikh within the community. Those who came from India, principally the Punjab and in the main from a village background, who were relatively poor back home, have come here with the expectation of doing better for themselves. The parents, many of whom might not be particularly literate themselves, indisputably want their children to be so and to do well. From that point on there is a lot of pressure on the children to succeed and achieve. Nearly all see the sense in this and

Huddersfield's Sikh Temple.

there is hardly any resentment. Also, there are those Sikhs, already well educated, who have either come from India or other places like Kenya. Together with these are those who were born, bred and educated here and for whom the value of education is both obvious and an imperative. On those terms, they will profoundly promote education within their own families. So, I think it is fair to say that the Sikh community places great value on education and much of this has to do with our cultural and religious background.

In the old days, before the establishment of our religion, there was a caste system wherein it was only the upper classes who could receive education, the lower classes being denied. Any reading or writing to be done would require you to go to someone who was literate and who would charge for it. Our gurus taught that education is everybody's birthright, so in that respect it is inbred in us.

My wife, Jasfal, was also born in Kenya. After I finished my education here I went back, my family had found this wonderful young lady and we were married soon after. Jasfal had been on holiday to England a few times before we were married. About seven years before we were engaged she came to a family wedding in Birmingham. We would eventually make our home here in this town. Huddersfield is where we live and we are not the sort of people who look back at something we have left behind.

Kenya is a very beautiful place and it was a very good place to grow up in. I do feel that kids here don't have the kind of freedom we had in Kenya yet in those four years I spent here in my early childhood, Britain was a very different place to the country we have today. We played around in the streets without any danger and there was none of this hooliganism and wanton destruction of property. Nowadays, you can see telephone booths kicked in and completely wrecked, paint daubed everywhere. There was none of that back in my childhood days. You know, I came to Essex, a county that is supposed to be one of the most racist places in the land, yet I never experienced any of that. Even in Romford, which was reputedly a strong haven for the National Front at that time, I never felt threatened or intimated. In fact, throughout the twenty years I have lived here I have never experienced any discrimination directed at me personally.

It took Jasfal about five, maybe six years to get used to life in Huddersfield. She never knew any neighbours, unlike in Kenya; also, the weather really took some getting used after the climate of East Africa. Jasfal said, 'I was initially depressed but then started studying and kept myself busy. Now, after settling here, with the children at university, if I was given the chance to go back, I wouldn't.'

Family

Our daughter is reading MORSE, which is Maths, Operational Research, Statistics and Economics. She wanted to become an actuary when she first started but has since had second thoughts. Our son started reading mechanical engineering last year but has now changed to accounts and finance. The science side, you see, is still strong and hopefully they will have good careers. However, the trouble is that the UK economy has changed from its industrial/sciences base to being far more service-related. There seems to be less demand for the sciences than there was in the past but we need to manufacture, we can't just rely on public services. If we want our country to have a strong, enduring economic base we have to have manufacturing, we need to train our young people in the sciences and technologies. Not everybody, of course, is geared up to being an academic: some people need to do things with their hands, but the opportunities to do that in this country are fast diminishing.

I do wonder what would happen if there were another world war. In the Second World War the manufacturing sector was stripped out and re-machined for the war effort, to make fighting aircraft, tanks, ships, etc. We simply can't do that anymore. Even the ammunition used by our armed forces is largely made abroad.

The old British Empire, as it was, set up an 'ideal', and so many people looked up to that and, even now I think, even today, if you go to the countries where the British Raj existed, the British way of life was the model and they try to emulate it. In many respects, they are probably more successful in maintaining that way of life than we are today in this country. In other words the traditional British way of doing things is admired and maintained perhaps more painstakingly and punctiliously in the old Empire, the modern Commonwealth, than it is here in what was the imperial heart and home land.

I think the thing that is good about this country, and continues to be good, is that for people who want and are determined to work there is the real chance to make something for themselves. It is a fair society and I don't think you have that kind, that level of fairness anywhere else. Even in Kenya, where I was born and where I grew up, there are tensions. Even in India I don't think there is the fairness in society we have here. If people really want to do something positive and worthwhile there are given every opportunity. People who are slackers are also given every opportunity, how could any society be fairer? Corruption is not rampant here at every level, in so many other countries it is. Go back to Kenya and straight away you are hit by the corruption. Come out of customs and immediately they expect something. If you want to arrange a party at home you've got to let the police know. You don't have to deal with this in daily life here.

One of the reasons why I live in Huddersfield is that for me it is a much nicer place than Leeds or Bradford. I think that Leeds has had its heart ripped out by development and Bradford is too depressed, I don't like the place, despite having worked there for twelve years. Huddersfield has a charm about it: two minutes and you are in the country. I am not so much a person who goes out socialising with other people a great deal but I do like to have an environment where I can go out to enjoy the landscape, the views, all of what nature can offer you. As far as the town itself is concerned, I think of all the five major towns in West Yorkshire Huddersfield is probably the best laid out. So much of its architecture is impressive, particularly the railway station and the structures in the area surrounding it. We've also got a good mix of shopping facilities, you don't have to go far to get most of what you want.

Both of my children were born here and they went to Moldgreen Primary and then up to Almondbury High for their secondary education. They concluded their secondary taking their A levels at Greenhead College, Almondbury being a feeder school to the college. We toyed for a while with the idea of sending our kids to public schools but my own background suggested otherwise: I went to a government school in Kenya. I believe that if children genuinely want to study they can do it in any environment. The problem of lack of respect in schools could be addressed. If discipline is taught at an early age and, equally if not more importantly, sustained, then it shouldn't be that difficult. If you don't catch the child early, it's very difficult to impose discipline later on.

The other side, of course, is the environment at home. Unless parents take a very active role in disciplining their children, it is futile to expect it to come from elsewhere. Unfortunately, far too many parents in this day and age choose to throw everything onto the state, i.e., it's the government's problem. There is a saying in Punjabi that if you don't have to pay for something, you don't value it. Education had to be paid for in Kenya, it wasn't free. You valued what you were receiving: it was a commodity you were buying. If all parents in this country had to pay for education and also the damage caused by some children then we would see a much more responsible attitude.

There are legal ways of addressing the problems but it will require some mettle from the government to do this. Many would argue in favour of the reintroduction of corporal punishment, even capital punishment, and the return of National Service. As I said earlier, we have so many problems whose cause is the lack of discipline and experiences like National Service did teach discipline. Currently, we have a minority of people who make a lot of noise while the silent majority would appreciate the reintroduction of many of the old ways.

You know, every child brings its own special gift. We have friends who have a Downs child and he is the most wonderful human being you could possibly meet. He seems to like everybody and is so appreciative of everything that people offer and do for him. My friends are people I have met either through the Sikh temple in Huddersfield or through my work. I tend to be a very private person by inclination but I do mix with people I admire and appreciate. I have been very lucky in that the vast majority of people I have met have been thoroughly decent, folk you want to associate with. So many of them do work for and contribute to the community.

I suppose us East Africans do tend to gravitate towards each other. Most East-African Sikhs live in the Leeds area but there are a few of us in Huddersfield and I guess I associate with them a lot. By the way, it is very easy for us to tell an East African from a Punjabi Sikh. We East Africans like to think we are a cultured lot but we're all Sikhs. Punjabi Sikhs in Huddersfield are from a variety of backgrounds and many of them are very well off. The work ethic is very, very strong amongst all Sikhs, the parents and grandparents providing the role models for the children. The push to success from the home is a permanent feature of Sikh life and there is no shyness of hard work. A lot of Indians who have come to Huddersfield have worked at the Hepworth Pipe factory, as taxi drivers and bus drivers, they'd work twenty-four hours a day if they could. Work hard, do well, make something of yourself is the goal. Having improved their lot, they send money they've worked hard to earn to their families back home. After five to ten years they hope to move into a small business, maybe a shop or taxi operation, always keen to go one better than the stage they're at. It all stems from the background of hard, grinding work back home.

The Great Game

David Gronow, Hon. Secretary of the Huddersfield Rugby League Players Association, together with David Weavill, Ken Boothroyd, Brian Curry and Derek Wroe, ex-players

It is indisputable that the contribution of Huddersfield to the game of rugby league is immeasurable. On the 29 August of 1895 the Northern Rugby Football Union, initially comprising eleven clubs from Yorkshire and nine from Lancashire, was formed at the George Hotel in Huddersfield, a truly illustrious moment in the development of a game that would become the Rugby Football League in 1922.

In the late nineteenth century Huddersfield was a major centre of the woollen trade and the dispute within the game stemmed from the issue of 'broken time'. The problem was that the mill owners wouldn't let their workers play football on a Saturday: if they did they wouldn't be paid. It wasn't necessarily an issue of North/South or class divide but the situation was different outside the northern industrial area. Undoubtedly, many people in the south in particular could afford to play rugby without suffering material loss. The same did not apply in the industrial north. The workers in Yorkshire and Lancashire couldn't afford to miss work and they worked long, hard hours, six days a week. Basically, that's why and how it all started.

The reduction in the number of players, from fifteen to thirteen, resulted from the change in rules required by the split from rugby union. It was to do with the structure of the union game, which remained the same while the new Northern Union continued to change its rules up till 1922 when the league was formed. They changed the number of points for a try, incorporated drop goals, did away with changing your numbers on the field, did away with the flankers and made six in the pack instead of eight, got rid of the line out. So, gradually the union game was phased out. The rules are still changing now, to make the game flow, to make it faster and to entice more people to come in. Up to the creation of Super League most teams were not fully professional. When myself (Derek) and David Weavill played we used to work five and a half, six days a week and then play on a Saturday. It was about 1974 when they started playing on Sunday and our first game was at Leeds. Then when Super League started most teams went onto a full-time basis, became fully professional. Full time is actually a condition of Super League. As to whether or not this was, in the first instance, purely a response to the high level of professionalism in the Australian game continues to be debated. Undeniably, a lot of the modern English rugby league if based on what has come from Australia. Super League now is a business, a very big business. Now Huddersfield has changed completely from running it as an amateur club into an organization with a totally business ethos and, no doubt it, Super League is the place to be.

I don't think that the two codes are so separate that if a player transferred from

The old ground at Fartown. (D. Gronow)

The George Hotel, where it all started.

The 'Team of all Talents', 1914/15. (D. Gronow)

one to the other he would have to relearn or for that matter learn a totally new game (DW). For a start, rugby union has always claimed to be an amateur game but, equally, there was always a profound belief within the league that there was money in union. So, as far as we are concerned it was never a totally amateur game. For example, how would you induce an international player to travel hundreds of miles every week to play club rugby without paying him – one way or another? 'Summat in the boot', as we would say.

Prior to Super League there was never a lot of money in league. In the seventies we used to play for £20-25 per game. Compared to your wage at work it was a good bonus. When I signed at Huddersfield we got £17 for a win and £7 for a defeat (DW). When I signed on it was £10 for a win, £5 for a defeat, winning pay if you drew away, losing pay for a draw at home (BC). The reason why a lot of rugby league teams in the fifties, sixties and seventies were successful was sponsorship, e.g. St Helen's and Pilkington Glass. It's obvious: the bigger your sponsor, the more you have to spend and the more you have to achieve success. Unlike your Batleys and your Dewsburys, they had little money and would suffer the consequences (KB).

There is still a big schism between rugby union and rugby league. If some player decided to come north to play rugby league he risked being ostracized by the union: David Watkins was a case in kind and Jonathan Davies were the same. My grandfather, Ben Gronow, played for Wales in 1910. He were the first man to kick off Twickenham. He came up here and signed for 120 gold sovereigns to play for Huddersfield. He were a stone mason, had a trade, and they found him a job and a house. He played for Huddersfield for about eighteen years and toured Australia twice. When he retired he left the club and went to coach rugby union at Roundhay, in Leeds, and there was a big row about it. The local MP in Huddersfield took up the matter. Roundhay had issued a centenary brochure with my grandfather at the end of line of the team photograph and identified as A.N. Other. They wouldn't name him because he had played rugby league, and that's how the union treated the players who, in its eyes, had transgressed.

On the other hand, if you played league you weren't allowed to play union. So, when we finished playing for the day, we all trooped up to Huddersfield YMCA, which is of course union, and if you wanted to play, it would be along these lines: Brian Curry became Brian Murray, Rob Valentine was A. Scott. Thus we came with our own ringers. Of course, what we really went for was the social side, the union always had a better social side than we did but that said, we had us own supporters' club and it were terrific. Nowadays, we've got Super League but as far as I'm concerned the fans have been ostracized: socially they're not allowed in with the players as they used to be. It's getting to be more and more like football, no intermingling of speccies (spectators) and players like it was in the past (KB).

The principal objective of our association, which has been going now for twenty-seven years, is to uphold the great tradition of Huddersfield Rugby League. We are on good terms with the club, we relate to the club and they with us, we get concessions and Mr Davy, who is the chairman, is a great traditionalist yet has very forward-looking views, which is why Huddersfield is still in Super League. Our determination is to never let the feeling go from this great club; it never will go (DG).

As it moves towards the football-style scenario the game will tend to lose a little of its past integrity. When you used to go to Fartown all those years ago as a speccie, you could lean on those railings and you could swallow the liniment, you could hear everything, the good and cross words, you were part of it. That was part and parcel of our game, and that's what's gone at Super League level. It's a total business now – get 'em in, get some money off 'em, get 'em sat down, buy 'em a whistle, let 'em all go home. Post match, how much does anyone care about speccies any more? They've paid once and if they want to go into the bar where the players go they've to pay again and to me that isn't right (KB).

One of the pleasures of this job I have is meeting people who've become outstanding. I've been a follower of rugby league since my dad took me along when I was in short pants and socks, and now meeting these Huddersfield guys from all generations is just enthralling for me. They all tell good tales: some of them are even true. They're a different breed, these guys, I like being with 'em, they're invariably forthright, occasionally can be brutal. They're straightfor'ard enough, a spade's a spade, that's how we are. They are always happy to acknowledge others who've played a part in their success, they're part of a team, the team is all-important. Through the years, these are the lads who have made Huddersfield what it is today: they have been the bedrock for the thousands of us who went through the turnstiles and the thousands more who followed Huddersfield's progress through the media. No plastic seats in those days: we stood or sat on wood, frozen to the bone, and we read about their exploits in the paper. At the end of the day, I was just wide-eyed as a kid, all my family was playing, and I still look on these lads as something different. We're all proud that we've been involved with the club. Case in point, we all went down to Twickenham for the final and even though we lost, well beaten in the end but it was a great effort for the club to get there. Now, they've some good players (DG).

The Giants, Twickenham, 2006. (D. Gronow)

Looking at the difference between a club like St Helens and ourselves, for a start they'll regularly have more people through the turnstiles. Then there's salary capping as well as gate receipts and the more commercialized your operation the more money you'll make. At the end of the day you are allowed to spend a certain percentage of what you make. Therefore, the clubs which make the most can spend the most. The determiner is how many people are coming through your gates and this is where your problem lies, for example clubs like Saints, Wigan and Leeds are getting crowds of 14-17,000, while Huddersfield are getting about 5,000. That's why the small clubs will never get into the Super League, they haven't the gate receipts. If I won £25 million on the lottery I could go to Huddersfield ('Get a round in first': DG) and if I gave them £20 million they couldn't go out and spend it on players because it's not earned money (KB).

When we moved from Fartown, we shared the old Leeds Road stadium with Huddersfield Town. During that transitional period we lost a hell of a lot of good will and a great many spectators. People hadn't wanted the move from Fartown, they very much wanted the money spending on the old stadium (KB). I think this new stadium has been a real boon for professional sport in Huddersfield (DW). There are still an awful lot of speccies, who've supported the club for twenty, thirty, even forty years, who were never happy about the move (KB). The other thing that upset so many supporters was the merger with Sheffield: it was never popular because of the strong local rivalry. It used to be principally with Halifax – Christmas Day, Boxing Day (DG).

As for the new names: Giants, Blue Sox, Rhinos, etc, when Murdoch formed the Super League, all the participating clubs got so many millions and it had to be spent on infrastructure, not your players, that was the main criterion. The stadium had to be a place fit for human habitation – comfort, toilet arrangements up to

Fartown delights, 1974. (D. Gronow)

speed. It's fair to say that a club or two spent more cash on players than facilities; Huddersfield wasn't one of 'em (KB). The new names came from merchandising and sponsorship, very much in keeping with the Australian concept of business in sport. That said, when we went down to Twickenham, the supporters were chanting 'Fartown, Fartown', not 'Giants'. That shows the depth of attachment, not just to the old ground but to the tradition here in Huddersfield. Obviously the little kids have no memory of Fartown and they'll shout for Giants (DG).

I think the future of rugby league in Huddersfield is assured, especially with Ken Davy as chairman, a very honest man and very shrewd. He has endeavoured to do the best for Huddersfield, he lifted Fartown out of the mire, pulled them up by their boot straps, and he's done the same for Huddersfield Town FC. He has definitely put Huddersfield RL right back on the map, particularly when we got to the Challenge Cup Final and were right in the eye of the media, while at the same time we were in the midst of a relegation battle which we successfully fought our way through. There is a lot of optimism in the club and among the spectators: the whole area was buzzing when we got to Twickenham (DG).

The cross-Pennine rivalry will always be there, it'll never alter – White Rose against Red Rose. Sometimes we actually prefer Southerners to Lancastrians. I played with Warrington for a while so I've great memories of the combat (DW). You know though, no matter how much rivalry there is on the field between Yorkshire and Lancashire clubs, and there's plenty, we all get on famously off the field (KB). (The rejigging of the political boundary which dumped part of Lancashire into Cheshire is usefully ignored). The respective players' associations invite each other back and forth, there's a lot of good rivalry there, so many great moments recalled, all in the right spirit (DG). Memories of the old days – first scrum smelt like a brewery (KB). Game's changed of course, six tackles changed it and you've probably got second rowers and props who can run as quick as sprinters (DG).

D'ya remember the cross code game between Wigan and Bath? We always reckon that Jeremy didn't want to play in that one, might have spoilt his dashing good looks. And John Gallagher, the ex-All Black full-back, he didn't enjoy his first league run out for Leeds, reckoned it nearly killed him, all the running and tackling he had to do, most of it going backwards. We do think that union has developed a much more professional approach, much more akin to league. Their defences are a lot tighter and fitter now because so many of the coaches they have got these days are from league. Back in the 1960s you used to watch an international between England and Scotland and you'd be bored out of your brain because all they'd offer were couple of moves and kick it, another move, kick it – bore the pants of you. Now it's totally different and watchable as they play a much more open type of game, they play the ball and run the ball and they aren't looking to kick every two minutes. It's definitely the influence of the open, attacking play from rugby league (DG/KB).

The differences in the level of play between the two hemispheres are rapidly narrowing but it's fair to say that the Aussies still have the upper hand. The English game has certainly responded to the influence of Australian and New Zealand coaching. More and more English coaches, younger coaches, are now coming through, lads like Paul Cullen and, of course, John Sharp at Huddersfield. They have some really good ideas of their own. There's always the question of whether or not we've too many imports but if you look at any professional sport: rugby league, cricket, football, you'll find the overseas influence (DG). OK, but if you look at the set up, a club will have three teams: first team and senior and junior academy teams. You're only allowed to play so many over twenty-ones in the senior team. You've got a squad of twenty to twenty-four lads in junior academy and they know that if they're going to be good enough they'll go up to senior, but where do the senior academy lads go? You've got four or five positions in the first team filled by overseas players. If you've got a right centre who's come through junior and senior academy and the first team has an Australian international right centre, where's the lad going to go? So, the problem is that our youth are held back from being internationals, whichever Super League club they're in, because they cannot get a place in a given position when an Australian or another overseas international is occupying it. The club are paying the international £100,000 plus per season, they're not going to drop him for a young lad coming out of the academy. They won't have an expensive overseas player sat on the bench. One would imagine that these Aussie internationals are on top money, perhaps more than their UK contemporaries (KB). I don't doubt that this is a test of loyalty but we've one Huddersfield lad, the full-back Paul Reilly, who's just done ten years with the club and has had his testimonial. Testimonials seem to have become a thing of the past because no one stops long enough at one club, particularly these Aussie and New Zealand lads. I'm not saying they're not good players because they are very good indeed but, hardly surprisingly, they won't feel a natural loyalty to an English club, they're overseas players whose natural loyalty will lie elsewhere (DG).

The characters and the lighter side

We've certainly had some characters: Billy Thompson, the international referee, Jim Mills, the Van Bellens, you could go on. Frank Simpson once had an altercation at Fartown with this lad who was playing for Keighley. Frank was a big local lad, 6ft 3in., seventeen stone, and the lad went into him a little waywardly, knees. No whistle from ref, nor did he blow for a repeat infringement shortly afterwards. Frank had had enough and announced his intention to resort to ungentlemanly behaviour should there be a repeat. There was and he did. Frank went on his way to the tunnel before the other lad hit the floor. Doc Hooper, the team doctor, went on and said he'd never seen a face like it in his life, it was like the Pennine Chain. He said, 'I'm gonna stitch you up but you don't deserve it'. The lad didn't know where he was, what day it was. He'd been warned and a man who'd been warned once by Frank Simpson should've kept well away.

Billy Thompson was ref for a Warrington v Widnes do. As they walked through the tunnel behind Billy, the Wires captain lets out to Billy, 'He's just f★★★★★★' 'it me!', pointing to t' Widnes lad. 'Nowt to do with me', says Billy, 'we're not on t' pitch yet' (KB).

When Wigan got relegated to the second division they played us at Fartown and it were a rough game. Wigan singled out Tony Johnson, a police officer and the only coloured guy on the pitch, and they gave him some stick: that match is now known as 'pot black'. It was known by this name because every time Tony made a break they clobbered him, stiff arms, the lot. There was nowt racist about it at all, as Tony would tell you. It were just good-natured violence. Eventually it ended up with six being sent off. Maurice Bamford were coach, he took Tony off because he'd had that much punishment and he put Ian Hobson on. It were a right free for all, three sent off from each side (DG).

I can relate to TJ at another game, these are things you remember having been sat there watching. We were playing against Featherstone, we kicked off and Tony ran the length of their half, taking this ball in mid-air and scored, not a hand laid on him. He were a real top runner, were Tony (DG). Another Johnson, Jimmy, one of our props back in the 70s, stuttered and him and Dennis Fitzpatrick, a prop, came from same rough area of Sheepridge. Jimmy were getting roughed up every time they went down for the scrum, he got one every time. Jimmy got fed up and next scrum, when he went down he held this bloke's shirt, lifted him up and he said, 'Next time you f★..f★..f★..f★..f★..f★'. Well, scrum had broke, ball hadn't gone in and referee didn't know what were happening. Dennis were stood behind Jimmy and he said, 'Jimmy, if you're gonna f★★★★★★' 'it 'im, then 'it 'im. He were a powerhouse of a fella were Jimmy but he just stuttered (KB).

I tell you, a book I like reading was written by Maurice Bamford, he's actually written a couple of good books, and he relates who he thinks were good players, not necessarily top class but proper workmen, rugby league props, etc. Fellas he had playing for him. Maurice wasn't too fond of his mother-in-law who'd had a pacemaker fitted. Maurice found out that microwaves, in the early days, could interact with pacemakers. He told her what clever machines they were and offered to poach her an egg and within no time at all she wasn't feeling well and she said she'd have to go home. Micro were worth every penny, said Maurice (KB).

We had Alex Murphy coaching down here, coached us to third division championship. Murphy were sitting in dugout with Joe Naidole, Tom's son, and listening to him were an education. 'Joe, Joe, don't try and dance round 'em Joe, yer a big bugger, go through 'em, Joe, go through 'em. Joe.' Everybody in t' stand could hear him. Alec has him playing prop one day, Joe could play anywhere in t' pack and for whatever reason, decided to kick. Murphy jumped out of t' dugout with Terry Flanagan, 'What the f****** 'ell you do that for, you **********, etc.' He didn't hold back did Alex. Terry's trying to rein in Alex while Joe's kick bounced and it bounced right onto their twenty-five line. Well, their defence was well forward as Joe ran through to take the ball and scored. Alex jumps up, 'You can't beat f****** good coaching'. I says to him, 'If that hadn't 've worked out Alex, what would you've done?' 'He wouldn't have played for t'next month, I tell ya that!'

Alex is on the after-dinner circuit these days. He were a good player, played for Saints for ages (DG). Mrs Murphy used to frighten me, you didn't argue with her, no way. We were once playing at Featherstone, sat in t'boring directors' box. Sat further down among speccies were some Featherstone supporters, 'effing and blinding. Well, at half time, she'd had enough and tapped one of the worst offenders on the 'ead with a tightly rolled-up programme, and she were a reet Lancashire lass. 'If you swear in this half like you did in the first half, I'll shove this programme up yer nose, sideways' (KB). A lot of women go to the games nowadays and they're very knowlegeable about it. It's a much more a family game than football. When we were at Twickenham, we had claret and gold on, all the kids did, all waving their flags and blowing their hooters. Yet, in front of us there were some from Hull, at the back were some from Leeds, from Wakefield and Halifax, all wearing their own club jerseys. There's no animosity, on match days supporters from both teams intermingle, Salford, St Helens, whoever. There's so much banter and it's all good-natured (DG).

In the 70s when all t' football hooligans were on the go, when it were really bad, I went to a semi-final at Headingley: Widnes against Featherstone and it were a sell out, 24,000. I were in paddock with Paul Dixon and I looked round and there were about four coppers. In t' far corner of west stand there were summat going off and these three young constables started running along the track in front of us. The old sergeant behind 'em called out, 'Whoa, whoa, whoa, slow down'. 'They're fighting in the far corner'. 'Slow down, take yer time, by the time you get there it'll be finished. They'll sort it out between theirselves', and they did (KB).

Wherever you go, even when you go away, there's never any bother, there's always banter. Some clubs were renowned for aggravation in the past, Warrington had a reputation and Hull used to be notorious. When Ken Senior played he never let his wife go to Hull. My dad was playing for Huddersfield at Hull just after the war and they'd stayed on the pitch at half time, satisfied with having had a good first half, when a beer bottle flies past his head. He turned around and there's this old woman. She says to him, 'That'll teach ya t'ave a bloody good game' (DG).

In the mid-1960s they signed three Fijians and Eric Sellers, who had an engineering works in Huddersfield, found them work. He found one lad a labourer's job, sweeping shop floor. One day Sellers were down t'side of the filthy old canal in the bottom of Huddersfield when Ken Senior went to see him. He asked where the lad was: he was out on the canal side with a knife tied

Fijians at Fartown, 1966. (D. Gronow)

to a brush handle, looking for fish. 'What the bloody 'ell are you doing?', says Ken. 'I spear', says the lad. It was a real culture shock for those boys when they came over. Playing on rock-hard grounds in winter in the freezing cold. I once went to watch Halifax and there was an Aborigine playing for 'em at full back, Joe Kilroy, and he were a good 'un. This day they were playing Hull Kingston and it was an absolute freezer up there. The wind and snow were blowing straight down the ground. For about three-quarter of the time Kilroy were stood behind a post trying to get shelter. They had to take him off, he'd bloody near hypothermia.

In the mid '60s, there were Huddersfield, Rochdale Hornets and Blackpool Borough all signing Fijians. Huddersfield also signed players from Wales and Scotland, from all over really, now it's very difficult trying to get them together for reunion dinners. Still, we do quite well, out of an attendance of about 300 for each dinner, probably about 100 are ex-players. That's what it's all about, getting them all together. It was different for teams like Batley and Dewsbury who got all their players from the heavy-woollen district (DG).

My grandfather, Ben Gronow, used to tell me the tale. Huddersfield had an awesome pack at the time he was playing, they were known as the 'team of all the talents', they won all four cups. York was another side with a big pack, lots of them were policemen and the tale concerned the two teams. The word was that York were out to 'get' Huddersfield and when they went down in the first scrum and my granddad said to the York lads, 'right lads, how

Ken, Dave and David, Cowcliffe Lib, 2006.

do you want it today, rough or smooth?' No problem after that, all went smoothly (DG).

A lot of these ex-players used to do the circuit as after-dinner speakers. They all had the stories, they pinched 'em, borrowed 'em, embellished 'em, yet they were all great stories you could relate to, might be a little bit o' truth in 'em., it's part and parcel of rugby league. What we do now at Giants with the ex-players at every home game is to bring one on to pick the half-time draw winning ticket. We'll bring a lad on who'll have played as far back as the '50s, the speccies appreciate it when he's introduced to the crowd and it's a way of keeping the younger supporters in touch with the players of old, who made the club great. We try to intermingle players from various decades from the '50s up to the turn of the century (KB).

There used to be a tradition among some of the supporters of going to watch Fartown one week and Town the next but admission prices now have stopped a lot of that, folk simply can't afford (KB). Certainly within my family the support for Fartown has carried on through the generations. I went with my dad, then my sons and my daughter went with me, and now their kids go as well. We've had an association with the club since 1910 when my granddad came up from South Wales. My father and my uncles all played for Huddersfield (DG).

Huddersfield's beautiful countryside

Liz Colquhoun, Kirklees Countryside Volunteer

I ended up in the Huddersfield area by pure accident really because in 1964 I had gone overseas to Jordan as a volunteer and spent a year out there. It was extremely interesting and I came back with one of the other volunteers as a boyfriend. We got engaged and married quite quickly. Ian was a mechanical engineer and was now looking for a job. My family was in Yorkshire and I came home to a temporary job in a girls' approved school in Wakefield. Ian's permanent employment could have been anywhere in the UK, his family were in Northern Ireland. He landed up with David Brown's in 1965 as a training officer, very much in vogue at the time, the government set up a new initiative as we were so far behind the Continent at the time in terms of vocational and industrial training. We were married at Christmas that year.

He was based at Durker Roods, which was DB's central staff headquarters. David Brown was quite an empire then, historically their apogee because they owned Vosper Thornycroft, Aston Martin and several other companies. Locally, of course, it was tractors and gears and he was more or less responsible for setting up programmes for the graduate intake, which he thoroughly enjoyed. For the time being it meant that I could stay at the school in Wakefield but I was hoping to get into social work. Huddersfield didn't have any vacancies which with hindsight I think was fortuitous, so I went into teaching and did a couple of years in Barnsley. I was teaching Geography at all levels at the Girls' High School, without a teaching certificate which wasn't required in those days. It was very interesting though it stretched me enormously. The education authority was very good as it credited my social-work diploma as a half of an income supplement, compared with a postgraduate teaching certificate.

We initially rented a cottage on the Woodhead Road in Holmfirth for 17s 6d a week. It had only one cold tap in what passed for a kitchen and it was on the bank of the river, just opposite the Victoria pub. A fortnight before we were married we were scrubbing the place, and it rained all day. Every so often my brother remarked, 'The river's rising, it's coming up the wall of the house Liz'. Houses close to us were being flooded and that was the day the river undermined the new car park in Holmfirth. Ever since I have been aware of the power of the river Holme and would not want to live on the valley floor. We then decided to move to a little detached house with a big garden in Upper Cumberworth for the frightening sum of £3,300. Above the tree line, above the snow line, at the top of the hill we got the wind four square from every direction. I stayed there for twenty-six years actually and we would raise our children there. Now, we continued to use the shopping and social facilities of Holmfirth, it was very drab and dreary in those days, absolutely West Riding personified. I was happy with that as my mother was born and raised in Bradford and I felt at home immediately. Ian found Holmfirth wet and snowy, in those days. Exploring the wider area we discovered Manchester as an exciting city and we booked tickets to go to a Doyly Carte production. It was in April and it began to snow in the afternoon and by the time we got home from work it should have been perfectly obvious that we weren't going to Manchester. Ian said that we were going to try and we set off up Greenfield Road. Joke! I don't think we got as far as The Ford Inn. You wouldn't think twice about such things now.

Once both my sons were at school, I got a part-time job at Penistone Grammar School, teaching Geography again. I stayed there for fourteen years but during that time Ian died suddenly – he was forty-four. Family, friends and colleagues were marvellous. There were ups and downs but we managed. Then, in 1987, all the part-timers at school were laid off. Help! What next? I was lucky and found a job in the Tourist Information Centre in Holmfirth. It proved to be far more varied and interesting than I could ever have expected – sociable too. I met lots of interesting local people there and learned a lot.

Now, you can't be a Geography teacher without becoming immersed in your local area. To understand the geography, you have to understand the history behind it, history, as I see it, being a summation of bits of geography. Industrial and land-use patterns change, and so on, and I always loved the historical background to what I was teaching. There I was at the tourist information office and that was an absolute gift. I had to deal with maps, had to order and sell OS maps and I'm crackers about them. Handling them and explaining to people exactly which ones they needed, well, bliss! All human life is there in a tourist information office. The wonderful thing was that nearly everybody said thank you. After a comprehensive school, aside from some intensely grateful parents, this was a gratifying experience. I used to go home dizzy, punch drunk. There were two of us on a job share and when we locked the door at 5.15 p.m. that was that, no preparation necessary as you had no idea what would happen the next day. You might be caught out but Sue, my colleague, and I always said that we may not know everything but we would damn well find out. It was a challenge and it was fun. It paid half as much as teaching and gave twice the pleasure.

The important thing, and I think it was one of the reasons why I got that job, was that several years earlier I was at Marsden Tunnel End doing a walk on my own and I saw a notice about working as a countryside volunteer. This was twenty years ago in the dying days of the county of West Yorkshire. I thought I'd like to learn to dry stone wall, I'd like to learn to lay a hedge, to put something back into the countryside. I very quickly discovered that I was more interested in exploring new footpaths and developing a concern for their well-being and survival than I was with the hard work of work parties. I began leading my own guided walks and that meant exploring more and more new footpaths and giving thematic, historical, environmental commentaries on the walks. I dipped into the local history libraries just to acquire more information and so it has continued, I've never looked back over the last twenty years.

In the early '90s, Kirklees had an environment or green fortnight, when John Harman was council leader and making a big name for himself in environmental circles. It was the birth, if you like, of green awareness and Kirklees was boasting that it was the greenest council in the land. I went to a meeting in Stocksmoor village hall about the Penistone line and out of that was born the Penistone Line Partnership. I wasn't a particularly frequent train user but was aware of their importance, we'd lost the Holmfirth branch line the year Ian and I moved to Holmfirth. As a result, myself and the chap who founded the partnership, a Lancastrian, Paul Salveson, dreamed up the train walks. Paul's whole life seemed to have been spent getting initiatives in public transport. He and I led the initial walks and we gradually gathered a few more like-minded people and the walks have continued. We've occasionally been a bit pushed for leaders but we do get people from as far afield as Lincoln as, until very recently, the service ran through to Lincoln. The line was their way to the hill country, of course, and they now have to make a connection at Sheffield. We don't get as many of them now but they've been a marvellously dedicated bunch. We've had walks the length of the line, even into Lincoln itself. Industrial archaeology is just scattered along the line.

In 1990, I had been a volunteer for about four years and I was getting exasperated and astounded by the number of blocked footpaths, and by the total lack of any maintenance along these paths. We thought this was wrong. There was no budget at all for maintaining and enhancing the rights of way network. The ramblers were pretty frustrated, as in fact was everybody I spoke to, while Kirklees was clearly neglecting this aspect of access to the countryside. This was definitely the council's Achilles' heel so we got a meeting together of the ramblers and bridleways groups, the latter particularly because of the lack of care of the precious few bridleways in Kirklees. We decided to hit the council, sending a letter to all seventy-two councillors explaining the situation, saying, 'What do you think?' I think we got about five replies. Then we got ourselves a name, the acronym ARROW for Action for Rural Rights of Way. Someone else suggested CROW – Country Rights of Way but we felt the former was harder hitting. ARROW started in March 1990 and we've come a long way since then. One very sympathetic councillor asked to organize the facts and point the council in the right direction.

We subsequently produced a report called *The State of Our Rural Rights of Way*, quite a major piece of work with colour photographs of disasters on the ground. We did a couple of surveys and we quoted the Colne Valley Society which had done its own several years before, working toward the same end. They had sent it to Leisure Services but action had not been taken. We logged the number of missing signposts, blockages, paths no longer walkable and then did some research around the other local metropolitan authorities: how many rights of way staff they employed; what their rights of way budgets were, etc. A lot of telephoning, a lot of work, putting together a table and whether you measured it in pounds per mile of right of way or per member of population, Kirklees wasn't just at the bottom of the scale, it wasn't even on it! It was truly bad news: we sent a copy to every councillor, the local MPs, the local press and we began to get somewhere.

So, ARROW took over our lives, it's a unique organization, no constitution, no elections. By summer of 1992 they appointed three or four rights of way staff. We thought we'd stick around for a while to make sure the right work was done and here we are in 2007 still hassling, still campaigning for more money. The rights of way unit has trebled in size. The maintenance of the way network is a legal obligation, a statutory duty of the council and all the procedures around rights of way: diverting; adding ways to the map; occasionally extinguishing one, are extremely legalistic and, as are all highway matters, ringed by legal procedures and restrictions. I think it's heartbreaking work for the RoW staff because they never have enough money and the ways are under constant threat, mainly from development. With every new housing and road development we lose more fields, another stretch of bridleway and footpath swallowed up, a bite at a time, here and there – tarmac rules OK! We monitor all planning applications that affect a right of way and argue for its preservation, not for its incorporation as part of an estate road but to be kept separately as an off road, tarmac free, pedestrian facility.

The interface now between the public and the council is the public right of way forum, held every three months and chaired by a senior councillor: the issues go back and forth. We use a provision within the law that requires a developer to make some local improvement as part of the planning bargaining, i.e. provide some green space. So, we can possibly get some improvement to rights of way through and around the development and it's in the developer's interests as they can advertise wonderful new housing with walks from the door. Just seeing nettles and brambles blocking paths can be very off-putting to folk buying new houses.

In the meantime we stayed at the family home in Cumberworth until my younger boy was at university, the older having already graduated. I was obliged to rent and I got a farm cottage in Honley, a bit small but the location was so delectable plus there was an unused barn at the side where we stored spare goods and chattels. We stayed there fifteen months and I was able to pay the rent from the sale of the house without reducing the capital – try that today. We were very happy there; it looked out across fields to Castle Hill, just so peaceful, magical. Now I live in my own house. When I moved here I had seven immediate neighbours over the age of eighty, only one left, must be a healthy area.

The beauty of Huddersfield's countryside is its variety. I'm particularly in love with the Holme Valley and more so with its upper end. Even up there you'll find history, abandoned farms and drowned valleys. When you walk at Bradshaw, beyond Digley reservoir, you can't help but be aware of a life that's gone. When Ian and I first walked it there were far more derelict farms which have, one by one, been demolished and I'm not quite sure why the last two have been left to stand there. I've always been given to understand that it was a condition of the appropriation of the land by the Huddersfield Water Corporation that all buildings were to be demolished but these last two weren't. We've had battles royal in recent years to prevent Yorkshire Water plc, a private concern, from redeveloping those. I hope we've seen that one off, there were two public enquiries into this and Peak Park has been very firm, they've just said no, as did two inspectors at the public inquiries.

Over the last couple of years we've had access to areas previously denied. As long as I've lived here I've heard folk ask why can't we get up Ramsden Clough, it used to be a ramblers' paradise. Then it was all shut off by the water authorities. I think that before and possibly even after the war, the people of the valley could go up there. There was no progress made on this issue until the CROW legislation. Now, of course, we can walk up the clough and around the hills at the top of the valley, it's such wonderful country. If you want a taste of wilderness

Above the Colne Valley, 1999. (L. Colquhoun)

it's up there, spectacular landscape and I prefer it to the Colne Valley which has more scattered farms, many of which have a certain degree of rural dereliction. The Colne was much more heavily industrialized and densely settled. I also love the countryside in the Denby Dale, Kirkburton and Cumberworth, where you are on to a different geology, off the millstone grit and on to the coal measures. It's a softer sandstone and has much lower rainfall, a gentler relief towards the eastern fringes of the Pennines. A lovely pastoral landscape of rolling countryside and amazingly well wooded in places. Gentler walking country than the Holme Valley, it has a wonderful network of footpaths, many of which are comfortably walkable. You get huge wide skylines offering vast south-Pennine panoramas.

I have a friend, a retired planning inspector, who always found Emley Moor mast an eyesore but for me it's a focal point on the skyline. When we lived at Upper Cumberworth the mast was always the centrepiece of our view. We got all the weather, we saw it coming, especially when it came from the north, and I shall never, ever forget the collapse of Emley Moor mast because the weather was so appalling. We had some horrific winters during the first fifteen years at Upper Cumberworth, we were just fractionally below the 1,000 feet contour. It was March 1969, nobody actually saw the mast come down as we were sheathed in freezing fog for three days and we had freezing rain throughout that time. All the power lines came down, we were without electricity for forty-eight hours and I had a four-month-old baby in a house without any heating except for a gas cooker. I had to

Winter, 2003. (L. Colquhoun)

cook for a neighbour who was all electric and our windows were solidly iced up; the high untamed privet hedge out the back simply lay down, along with the new birch trees we had planted, with the weight of the ice. The whole lot were frozen to the ground, it was bizarre. The eastern windowless wall of the house was encased in about four inches of solid ice as the wind was in the east. It wasn't until power was restored and we got our radio back, no telly in those days, that we discovered that the mast had fallen. What experiences the engineers must have had don't bear thinking about, they were working round the clock. One of the mast cables had snapped under the weight of the ice, that's what caused the collapse. Holme Moss had to be closed for obvious reasons, the same type of lattice mast. That was certainly a seminal moment in my life. For those few days it was a very strange life indeed and it taught me a lesson.

In later years when Kirklees got a snow blower, it would come up and go through the huge drifts. There was an incident when the blower was going past the Sovereign and it suddenly started blowing bits of metal. Somebody had been forced to abandon a sports car at the side of the road and a few bits and pieces came off before anybody knew what was happening. That was the story anyway. I can remember one winter night when I wanted to go for a walk over the fields in the dark. Hugh, my oldest, came with me and it was absolutely scary. We were struggling in the snow, it was pitch black and it was snowing. Two or three fields from the roads and lights were no longer visible but we hit a lane and walked down to the road but it was heavy going. Snow down our wellies, if I'd been on my own I'd have been terrified. That was December 1981 and it hasn't happened since really. We've had the odd day but nothing prolonged, the great snows have gone.

As a Kirklees Countryside Volunteer I have led several hundred walks. We do a six-month programme, twice a year, and I might have four or five walks in each programme, then I do more walks for the Penistone Line Partnership and an occasional extra walk, e.g. for the South Pennine Walking Festival. Between us volunteers we lead about fifty walks a year, probably more, and I've been a member for twenty years. Originally, we were the West Yorkshire Countryside Volunteers, run from Wakefield and covering the whole of the county. Added to this all walks have to be pre-walked and each leader has to have a back up. I do come across so many people on the walks and almost without exception they are very pleasant. That said, you will find folk who simply assume that the walks will always be there and the leading and the map reading will be done for them.

Nonetheless, it is rare to find someone you cannot cater for. It's not unusual to have fifty people on a walk, especially if it's a theme walk. We've had huge numbers on our railway branch line walks, including all sorts of people from outside the area. It can be quite unwieldy, particularly keeping to the actual right of way. No more than two abreast, nothing more inflammatory to a farmer than a horde of people tramping across his fields, but walkers are generally very good about this. The weather, of course, has to be borne. It's not uncommon for me to get to a spot and say that on a good day, usually the day of the pre-walk, you can see this, that and the other, but today, nowt. Of course, the other way round happens with the same regularity. At least folk realize that all walks are pre-walked. Everything really needs to be planned as best as one can, pit stops for food and for the loo. That this is accepted without complaint is one of the reasons why I continue to do it. There are an awful lot of people out there who enjoy this and many of them make friends, it's a social occasion. As they grow in confidence they'll join the ramblers or another group, or go off walking on their own or in small groups. Thus we measure our success.

Those who like long, hard walking are catered for elsewhere: our job is to introduce people to the rights of way, linking ARROWS work with guided walking. We can and do choose footpaths we want people to know and use and we will take a group along it to do a bit of clearance on paths that are semi-overgrown or blocked. Occasionally we have to turn to the rights of way unit and tell them if a path is impassable. Hopefully they can expedite its clearance. I have to admit that I do preach about footpaths on my walks. I say to people that if we don't use, look after and fight for our rights of way then where will our children and their children walk? Our rights of way are being relentlessly eaten away by building development; add to that damage from weather – rainstorms washing away bridleways and leaving them unfit for use; add to that diminishing rights of way budgets in a society where far too many people don't want to pay any tax at all; add to that stroppy landowners who obstruct and get away with it because councils can't always be persuaded to take them to court. However, the Rural Payments Agency has now brought in something called 'cross compliance': to earn your rural payment as a landowner or farmer you've actually got to abide by certain standards and conditions, including rights of way on your land. There is the distinct possibility that landowners could lose their payments if they obstruct rights of way. So, a malefactor could face not only the council but also the NFU.

What is really impressive about this area is how quickly you leave the town to find yourself in open countryside. One minute you're driving past terraced cottages up against mill chimneys, go 500 yards up the hillside and you hear the larks singing above winding country lanes. Huddersfield's industrial tentacles reached along the valley bottoms, leaving vast areas of open upland country. Go back to Phyllis Bentley, whom nobody reads these days, and recall that you could get on a tram on Sunday and you'd be out in the hills in next to no time.

Tales from a Kirklees TIC

A classic, one we all remember. It was a Saturday afternoon and we're really up-to-our-necks busy. A large and extremely aggressive gentleman came to the counter and demanded the name and address of the manager of the local. 'I suppose he would call it supermarket, hrrumph!' He was spitting with anger, I thought this bloke wants calming down as the rest of our clients drifted away and my colleague, unforgivable, nipped off to the stockroom leaving me well and truly stuck with it. It transpired that the supermarket was all out of pork pies at 2.00 p.m. on a Saturday. He was crimson, spluttering and hugely overweight and I was anticipating his heart attack. I suggested that they would not be keen on overstocking at the weekend as they would be closed on Sunday. 'Let me tell you, I run my own shop and I never run out of anything! They're all the same', as he regaled us with a story of his being obliged to tackle some unfortunate in Sainsbury's. He had demanded to see the manager but was met by the grocery manager, who was 'some little cacky, jumped up ... something or other'. I said, 'Don't send me the monkey, I want the organ grinder. Would you believe it, they hustled me out and I'm still in legal

Above: Well attended at Upper Knowl, 2002.

Left: Liz.

correspondence with them'. More hrrumph! I gave him the address of the supermarket and suggested he write to them, and then he disappeared. People came of hiding from behind bookcases and my colleague tiptoed out of the stockroom. 'Is the coast clear?' We still laugh about it. In hindsight, we perhaps should have backstaged him out of the public eye but let's face it, we were terrified. In truth, we rarely get aggression.

We were celebrating 'Yorkshire Day' and doing something different. I was dressed up as Nora Batty, rollers, pinny and de rigueur wrinkled stockings. It was chucking it down, a really miserable day and this middle aged couple came in. Obviously as miserable as sin, they mooched around and we gave out our cheery 'Hello, hello'. Ignored, they mooched some more and finally brought a postcard to purchase. We tried to cheer them up with happy chat, a total failure. My tatty ensemble failed to raise even a glimmer of a smile. 'It's a pity about the weather ... Yorkshire Day ....' Nothing, no response. We were giving away some knick-knacks in celebration of this special day. I explained, 'As it's Yorkshire Day'. 'Yorkshire Day?', they looked at us, mystified. 'Yes, Yorkshire Day', said Sue, 'that's why Liz is dressed up'. 'Dressed up?' 'Yes', said Sue, 'you know ... Nora Batty ... the television programme?' 'Oh, we thought you were going on somewhere after work'. Rollers in my hair because I was going out for the evening!!

There were always the impossible requests. Two middle-aged ladies, obviously on a coach trip, came in. 'Can you tell us how to get on to the moors?' 'Moors?' 'Yes, we want to look at the moors'. Well, I didn't know how to take this at all, they were in sort of crimplene skirts, poly blouses and ordinary shoes. 'Like the Bronte moorlands...and that, you know'. 'Well, there's nowhere within easy distance from here, you'd probably have to take a bus up the valley to Holme, and you can walk in from there. There are some nice little walks from the office if you don't mind going uphill'. Glum faces, peeved voices, 'No, we want the moors. We've only got an hour, then we've to go back to the coach. We want the moors'. 'Well, I'm sorry, I don't think we can help you with this one. We've got lovely hillsides, pastures and woods around us, lovely scenery that eventually fades into the moorlands higher up but I don't think you'll have the time to get there'. 'Oh ... right', and they walked. As they went out one said to the other, ' Ooh well, at Haworth you walk of the information centre and go straight on t'moors'. Sue said, 'I'm freeing you up for the afternoon Liz, get a spade and go'n move them damn moors'. It's just patience, you do need patience.

We had a lady come in. 'I want to know where the real Nora Batty steps are'. 'Yes, fine, we'll give you a leaflet, it's very easy, very near'. 'I've got the leaflet and I've been to where it says but those aren't the real ones'. Blink, blink, I checked she'd been to the right place. 'Yes, been there, but that's not where they film, that's just where you send the tourists, it doesn't look like that on the film. I've always watched it. Now, where are the real ones, please?' Well, what do you do? 'I don't know of any other steps they use, and I've seen them filming there'. No, wasn't having any of it. 'I know what you people do, you're just sending me where you send those tourists'. Hopeless.

Like the American lady who came in to book accommodation in 'Hayworth', not that uncommon actually. Usually we say something chatty like, 'You'll find when you get there the locals call it 'Howarth'. We do have some very charming and courteous Americans but this lady wasn't one of them.

We got the road atlas out and showed her the route and wrote it down for her. So, we get to Keighley. 'Keethley, Keethley, where's that. Oh, I see, you mean Keeley'. So I said, 'It's actually called Keethley, that's what you'll need to ask for'. 'Whadya mean Keethley? I don't see any TH in that word, it's Keeley', and off she went. A lot of the time it was learning to cope with serious misunderstanding and not letting your jaw drop.

It was about 10.30, a lovely sunny day in the school holidays. In came a couple of slightly giggly, youngish ladies, with two or three kids between them. 'Can you tell us where we are, we're not quite sure.' 'Well, you're in Holmfirth, where they film *Summer Wine*. 'Holmfirth, right … erh … we're trying to get to the Lake District.' 'Where did set off from?' 'Manchester, we must've got wrong road out of Oldham'. We tried to direct them, they had absolutely no idea where they were. It's reckoned that fewer than 15 per cent of the adult population can actually read a map properly, how true I don't know. A TIC colleague manning a mobile at Scotch Corner was confronted by a bunch of mums and kids who were completely lost. They were from the East Midlands, somewhere near Leicester, and were looking for Skegness. A husband of one had instructed them to turn right when they saw the sign. I guess people cope with life in their own way.

The Huddersfield Motor Racing Club

John Mitchell, a co-founder, and his wife Audrie

I was born in Sheffield in 1930, eventually moving to Crosland Edge in Huddersfield as my father was managing director of Brockholes Motor Company. I was sent to Giggleswick School on the edge of Settle in the North Riding and stayed there until I left to do my National Service. My father remarried but developed cancer and sold out to a chap in Huddersfield. He died in 1963 and with the funds I inherited I started John Mitchell Motors. I had actually started racing when I was sixteen.

I came back into Hudderfield after the Army, by which time my father had remarried. My mother married a colonel in the Army, they went out to Africa and she asked me to go with her but my father said that if I came to work for him he would give me a car – that did it. I joined the Motor Club when I was about twenty and we did a lot of rally work at that time. I was then invited by Ford to go down to Goodwood to test the new Anglia, the cut-back version. I had to do 10,000 miles in a week just going round the track. There were three Formula One drivers, Graham Hill, Roy Salvadori and Bruce McLaren, who were the principal test drivers and I got to share the testing with each of them in turn.

The Motor Racing Club was originally the Huddersfield Motor Club before a group of us translated it in 1959. We broke away from rallying to form a racing team. The club is still going but it isn't as we knew it. In fairness, the four of us were the sons of the owners of big motor sales and garage companies and we could pump quite a lot of money into the club. People can't afford to indulge that sort of thing anymore, it was an expensive hobby and there were never more than four of us in it. I kept it up but I had this premonition ever since I was eighteen that when I got to the age of forty I would either be killed or have a very bad accident. I had seen three racing drivers killed and this feeling kept returning, so when it got to the week before my fortieth birthday I sold the car. The chap who bought it from me came from Brighton and he took it to the Dutch circuit at Zandvoort and he was killed in it, three days after my birthday. It transpired that he had actually had a heart attack, so it wasn't the car. I naturally assumed that the car was written off but in fact it was taken to South Africa and repaired out there.

Four or five years ago the telephone rang one evening and it was this chap who had bought the car and was trying to trace me. He was going to a local race track and asked me if I would like to go to see him and the car. I met him and sat in the car again, after all those years. The car was a Brabham BT14 and the chap in the photo, Michael Scott, was still racing it and winning with it. He has since sold the car on. I actually went down to Silverstone to see Jack Brabham about the car. He told me that there were only fourteen of them made, my car had

John with Michael Scott and the BT14. (J. Mitchell)

been the eighth and it had just resold for £35,000. Nearly forty years before I had paid £1,500 for the same vehicle.

I literally raced every weekend and gained 150 first places. It was never lucrative: it was long before any form of sponsorship, we did it for the fun and the buzz. Our activities were of sufficient popularity with enough people to earn us a regular column, every Wednesday, in the *Examiner*. I have even raced a wooden car, a Marcus, the first of its kind to be made and I had Marcus No. 3. It was the brainchild of the chap who designed the illustrious wartime aircraft, the Mosquito. I took it over to Holland where it appealed to the Dutch with their fondness for wooden footwear. It was so light you could lift one corner to change a wheel, the heaviest part was the engine. They're still being made and I recall our engineering operation selling engines to them.

I did a lot of the tuning and we used to demonstrate down at the Sports Racing Car Show in London, taking our own cylinder heads. I remember being fortunate enough to have the very first E Type Jag in Huddersfield. When I left it the Racing Club came to an end, the founder members were now doing their own thing, so club racing had a life of about fifteen years. The existing club is interested in rallying rather than racing. Tony Lanfranchi continued to race saloon cars until he died about two years ago. The *Huddersfield Examiner* retains a record of all the information it published on the Racing Club and it would be nice if it could be filed and catalogued. I had intended to do it but open heart surgery has put all that sort of thing beyond me, I'm afraid.

Above: The four founders in 1959 outside Brockholes Motors, where Sainsbury's Shorehead supermarket now stands. (*Huddersfield Examiner*)

Left: Possibly heading for Le Mans. (*Huddersfield Examiner*)

Below: Not exactly Formula One. (J. Mitchell)

The four boys at Late Roundup in the Farnley Cock. (J. Mitchell)

Audrie

I first met John, whose wife I would eventually become, when I was seventeen. We met again by accident about twenty-five years ago, when he was about fifty and we were both on our own. Suddenly, there was something there that never had been before: we had just been pals in those early years. Yet, you know, I do in a way resent not being around him when he was racing. The stories he used to tell had me in stitches, now he can't remember them.

There's one interesting story I remember. John had been racing at Rufforth and was coming home. He was coming up Bradley Road and he approached some roadworks and in those days there would be a man in a hut with a brazier by the side of the hole. Nonetheless, in his E Type John drove straight into the hole, right outside where his rallying navigator lived. The headline in the *Examiner* told of the watchman's consternation. He thought a doodlebug or some such had landed in the road and as fast as legs would carry him he hared off over the hills. John recalled it: 'I had deliberately gone up Bradley Road because in those days it was unrestricted. I remember seeing this arrow not particularly pointing to where one ought to go. Too late did I see the hole and I was landed with a very large repair bill of £1,800. Huge enough today, it was frightening in those days. The four founder members, Tony Lanfranchi, Peter Kaye, John Hepponstall and myself had a do at The Golden Cock in Farnley Cock on my seventieth birthday. Sadly, we are now down to three'.

The Poles

za wolnosc wasja i nasja

For more than 200 years, 'For your freedom and ours' has been the slogan and battle cry of the Polish soldier fighting for the ever-elusive freedom of his nation. Forgetting the past is too readily used as an excuse when we can't be bothered to remember it or it becomes too much of an embarrassment. The debt of honour owed by this country to the men and women of the Polish armed forces still remains formally unacknowledged. The Poles were exceptional, and unique in the British experience of immigrants in recent times. They were a demobilised military force drawn from all three service branches and here because freedom in their homeland, for which they had fought so long and hard, was denied them.

Desperate to fight in the Battle of Britain but refused the opportunity before the 31 August 1940, the Warsaw Air Regiment, now 303 'Kosciuscko' Squadron, RAF Fighter Command, alone shot down 126 German aircraft for the loss of only nine of their own. In the battle of numbers and psychology the Poles were the crucial factor. Consummate air fighters, they hurled themselves with unrelenting fury at the Luftwaffe. It is conceivable that had they not been there the RAF might have been overwhelmed in the greatest air battle ever fought.

On the ground, the battle honours of the Polish Army, from Fort Westerplatte to Monte Cassino and beyond, are beacons to the dwindling minority who still choose to cherish duty, honour, loyalty and self respect in an age of hedonism and self indulgence. Nominally under French control General Sikorski, the Polish President and Commander in Chief of the Army refused to surrender when France capitulated in 1940; the Poles and their Chief came to England and began their long association with this country.

On the 1 August 1944, the men, women and children of the Polish civilian Home Army, the Armia Krajowe, buoyed by monstrous Soviet duplicity, rose up in Warsaw in an act of bloody defiance against the German Army. The Warsaw Rising was supposed to last only a few days: it raged for sixty-three. The flames of the funeral pyre of the city could be seen from the air in the night sky for over a hundred miles. With unbelievable courage Polish, South African and British airmen sacrificed themselves in the inferno as they attempted forlornly to supply the city. On the 2 October General Bor Komorowski surrendered the shattered remnant of the Armia Krajowe. Warsaw was destroyed and a quarter of a million of its citizens killed.

At the end of the war the conquered nations of Western Europe regained their freedom; the Poles lost everything except their faith and courage. With its opponents killed the Communist Lublin government declared that the city would be rebuilt but the price was Russian domination. General

August 1940; General Sikorski decorates the standard of the Polish Highland brigade after the Narvik campaign. (Anon)

Anders' soldiers were even denied the right to take part in the victory parade in London, Stalin's influence stretched that far. With the failure of all that they fought for a vast number of Polish servicemen and women remained in the UK, many of them making their homes here in the West Riding. Time has claimed most of them. Here are the voices of two who served their country and ours in Lieutenant General Anders' Polish 11 Corps, Italy.

Alex Plytnik, Soldier and a citizen of Huddersfield since 1948. After sixty years Alex still finds the English language really daunting

I have pictures of Poland before the war. I was in the Army, the uniform very different to the British Army. In Italy I served in the 7th Horse Artillery in the Polish Corps. I originally came from Northern Poland, a place called Suwalki, close to the old Russian (now Lithuanian) border. My father was a farmer and I grew up on a farm.

After the war, in 1946, I came to England from Italy. The only relative I had was my sister, who had lived in America since just before the war. My father had been in America with his brother but came back to Poland. His brother stayed there but I do not know what happened to him. My sister's husband, an American, had come to Poland to take her back there. She was older than me and has already died. I have never seen her again after she left Poland but she used to write and send photographs of her children.

The first place I came to in England was Morpeth in Northumberland. You understand I am still a soldier until 1948 when I was taken to Chester for demob. Then I came to Huddersfield to find a job. I worked as a weaver for John Crowther in Milnsbridge for about ten years and then I go into engineering with Brook Motors until I am made redundant. By now I have one child, my daughter. I am very proud of her and my grandchildren. My daughter was studying in Cambridge and is now in law. My older grandchild is a teacher and her sister is still at university until 2007.

When I first came to Huddersfield I bought a house in town, in Wentworth Street, near Greenhead Park but the house was too big for me. The house I am in now I had built by a fellow I gave £50 to as a deposit. I came in here about 1958/59. I am very happy here in England, it is the fairest country in the world and the English people are so good. If you have nothing and are poor, the government helps you. It is not like this in so many other countries.

After Brook Motors I stay here working in my garden, I am retired a long time. My wife was working in Lindley, in the infirmary. You know, in Poland people were so poor, they had nothing and they still seem to be poor. Why does the Englishman not go to Poland? There is nothing there for him. Some Polish woman says to me that all is better in Poland but I ask why are so many Polish people still having to come to England, why the English do not go to Poland. I don't think she likes me so much.

Alex in the Polish 11 Corps in Italy.

The English people do not think just for today or tomorrow but for the future, for a long time. I think it is only a matter of time before all the small countries over Europe, like Poland, Slovakia, Hungary, will speak English because the English people think ahead to the future, this is so important. Might be, the Germans and the Russians will not, I don't know, but all the young people want to speak English.

My wife is Italian and when the war was finished, General Anders said that any Polish boy who wanted to marry an Italian girl could do so. Before this it was not possible. I came to England by myself to make a little money to set up home. I have to find a job and then I am saving, saving. Then I go for a short holiday to Italy to my girlfriend's town and we get married. My wife lived in Osimo, near the Adriatic in Northern Italy. After we were married I brought her back to Huddersfield but we used to go back for our holidays to Osimo. I have never been back to Poland, I have no family there. Would there be anything there I would know?

Ever revered: Lieutenant General Anders on the wall of Janina's sitting room. (J. Stanowska)

Janina Stanowska, lorry driver in the 11 Corps and citizen of Huddersfield since 1946

I was born Janina Lukowska and I lived about 16 kilometres from the Russian border before the war, near a town called Kostopol, today some 150 kilometres into the Ukraine. I was eighteen when the Russians invaded; they came in the night, gave my family about two hours to get some clothes and food together, took us off, eventually to Western Siberia. The first stop was not far from Moscow where we were kept until the rivers were ice free and then we were taken by barge up to the taiga. The families were put into two empty villages, we found later that they and another village had been occupied by deported Ukrainians, Lithuanians and Latvians until 1931 when there was a vast famine. Nearly all these people died of starvation, terrible things were done. The survivors were put into one village and we were put into the other two. We were there for maybe a year, one day they just came and said, 'You are free, go!' Go where, we were 1,000 miles from Poland, how would we return? Yet a group of about eight men decide to go because winter was coming, if we stay we die from cold and hunger. So, they made a huge raft for seven families to go together. Just before we left a family from Poland sent us a parcel, it was just dried bread but it helped to keep us alive.

Days went by without count until we reached a village where we met a lorry driver who was so kind. He told us that

Janina in the Polish 11 Corps, Egypt. (J. Stanowska)

Her first husband, Julian Szymanki from Nowy Sacz, soldier in the 11 Corps. (J. Stanowska)

we had about one hour to meet a barque coming on the Volga to this river. We had to hurry and he drove all of us to meet the barque. We continued down the river on this boat, I can't remember how long, until we saw a Polish officer on the bank. People tried to stop us landing because of our papers but my father pushed them aside. The Polish officer told us that General Anders was close by and forming an army from Poles released from Russian captivity. The officer had been stopping all river traffic to find Poles and bring them ashore. Now we are in the Polish Army and we boarded a train to Buzuluk, east of Kuybyshev. Now I am in the ATS waiting to see how I will serve in the Army. Our President and our Commander, General Sikorski, came to Buzuluk, it lifted us greatly.

When I was in Russia, please don't laugh, I had a dream. I dream of a great eagle hovering over the earth, the eagle is the symbol of Poland. I feel that something is happening for Poland, though we were in the Siberian forests and we knew nothing, no news is coming through. I told my mother, 'I think some thing is happening for Poland' because of the dream. And it was at that time that General Sikorski was organizing the Army in England but I could know nothing of this. Now, in Buzuluk, the dream had come true. The Army now moved to Tashkent where we had a terrible time as we were struck by typhus. So many died. I had been trying to find my mother when I fell ill with typhus. I nearly died in the hospital but the man who was shaving my hair off, this had to be done, took my rosary from my pocket and put it in my left hand. After two weeks I become conscious and I find the rosary in my fist. I was now well and went back to my unit and the Army moved on to northern Persia (Iran), via Bukhara. We stay a short while in Tehran before going through Palestine to Egypt and then on to Italy and the war.

I am now a lorry driver for General Anders. We women drove to the second line during the terrible fighting at Monte Cassino taking ammunition, petrol, guns, water, food, blankets – anything the soldiers needed. There were no railways, these had all been bombed and destroyed, everything had to be moved by the roads which were very bad but the women were not allowed to go to the front line.

We women drivers were in Forli, the Polish Army had reached Bologna, when we heard all this shouting. The English and American soldiers are all happy, the war is ended and they will be going home. For us Poles it was different, our country was not free after all the fighting. What would happen to us, where would we go, we did not know. We could not go back, our homeland belonged to the Communists whose 'truths' were all lies. I had seen Communism first hand in Russia. While the fighting is continuing we have no time to think, only to do our duty. Now it is over and the girls are in tears. One of the girls got some wine and we got drunk. I have never been drunk before and I have to stick my head under water from one of the tanks we are carrying.

Her second husband, Adam Stanowski, soldier in the 11 Corps. (J. Stanowska)

While I was in Italy I got married to a Polish soldier. He was sent to England with the Resettlement Corps, I was now pregnant and joined him later in 1946, at a big camp near Market Rasen in Lincolnshire. The person who is the godfather of my child came to tell us that a Polish community is starting in Huddersfield. We can go to work in textiles. My husband, Julian Szymanski, (so I was Janina Szymanska) had gone to Derby, digging trenches for gas pipes, his hands are in a poor state – not used to heavy digging.

When we came here we lived in Hill Top in Slaithwaite and we worked for Crowthers in Crimble. They were very short of tradespeople so there was plenty of work. We bought a house there and to help us to pay our mortgage we had lodgers, Polish soldiers who are not yet married. After a while they went on short working so I start my gardening, growing the vegetables we need. I also used to bring pieces home from the mill to mend whenever this was possible. My neighbour taught me how to do this and I have to learn, we have to work to live.

I then said to my husband that we must find a smallholding with some land so I can

Waclaw, Janina's brother, killed in action serving with Bomber Command. (J. Stanowska)

Janina, 2006

grow much of what we need and perhaps keep a cow. So, we bought this place in Golcar which was a ruin. We had little money but the boss at Crowthers was a kind man who loaned us a deposit and took it from my husband's weekly wage. We moved in here in 1958, now I will only leave here feet first. My husband died suddenly of a heart attack and later I met another Polish ex-serviceman, Adam Stanowski, who was a widower and we were married but he too has died. I had three daughters with my first husband and seven granddaughters, nearly all have gone to university.

You know, we have been very lucky. After the war we had few choices, we could not live under Communism in any circumstances and England gave us a home. I still go back to Poland, I have been about five times, the last about five years ago. The first time we went back on holiday we were frightened even to speak because we were seen as the enemy, we had stayed in England. After that it started to get a little easier. It was odd because I always seemed to be there when the great events were taking place, it was not planned. I was there when the Holy Father was in Poland and when the great strikes led by Lech Walesa were happening in Gdansk.

We, the old ones, are fewer and fewer yet we have a very active club in Huddersfield. We are the largest European immigrant group in Huddersfield. Bradford has the biggest Polish community, even bigger than Leeds, and Halifax and Keighley have theirs. We all used to be the Polish Ex-Servicemen's Clubs, now we tend to be social clubs.

You know, I wondered what happened to all my family after Russia. My mother died there and I found out later that my brother was killed serving in a bomber squadron in the RAF. He is buried in the Polish cemetery in Newark and every year I go to his grave. My mother used to say to him that he would never die his natural death because he wanted to be everywhere, he was so active. The last time I saw him was in Russia and then they moved to Persia and he went on to a Polish squadron in England. My father was in the Army in Italy and he kept asking me if there had been any letters from Waclaw, my brother. The only news we ever received was the notification of his death, killed in action. He was such a fine fellow.

Geoff Hill

chairman of the 33rd/76th Duke of Wellington's West Riding Regiment Association

I was brought up in Almondbury but my father who was in the Territorial Army was actually called up a fortnight before war was declared, so the family went to live in Deighton with my paternal grandmother. We carried on living in the house after my grandma died. Dad, who served initially with the Dukes and later with the RASC, was in for the duration of the war.

I was called up on 1 February 1956, the day of the Suez Invasion. I thought, 'by heck, this is good timing'. I did my basic training at Halifax in November, then a week's leave followed by a posting to Cyprus. The battalion had been earmarked for the Suez operation but the whole thing, as you know, was aborted. So now it was internal security duties in Cyprus against EOKA and that's where I joined them. I was there for the best part of a year, we'd quite enjoyed it as we were young lads and up for a bit of action. We hadn't really felt in that much danger, I only saw one or two dead bodies.

Then we were sent to Northern Ireland which wasn't yet what it would become in 1969 but the signs were very obviously there. So it was no surprise when it did flare up. Police were heavily armed, stations sandbagged and adverts in the paper reflected their prejudices, e.g. 'wanted: milk roundsman, RC need not apply', or the other way round. Punch-ups in Londonderry Council meetings over gerrymandering, it was all going on. A local civvy who worked in our camp was a Protestant married to a Catholic girl. He said to me, 'D'you know Geoff, the milkman won't deliver my milk, mixed marriage a fatal error'. Another thing, when we first got there our padre gave us all a talk. He probably assumed we were all nominal C of E when he came along. The gist of it was that there were seven girls to every man in Belfast and all they want to do is marry a soldier, have as many children as they can and bring them all up as RCs. The Catholic lads in our unit took a dim view of this. The bigotry was there and it was very obvious.

Our job was to work in conjunction with the RUC when they were carrying out stop and search and we were there to guard them. Nothing untoward ever happened. Sometimes the police would ask a driver to step out of his car and open the boot. You might get, 'Now then lads, how are you enjoying yourselves over here?' Another time, the driver would scowl and spit. You knew which way the wind was blowing.

One time I got an unofficial commendation. I remember an Orange parade day, we had to guard this bridge into Londonderry, everyone was on duty. Orders were that nobody stops on that bridge, vehicles, pedestrians, didn't matter, just keep 'em moving. A car stopped just short of the bridge and three fellows got out and walked halfway across and stopped. I was the corporal and I said to a couple of our lads to tell these blokes to move on. I couldn't hear what was being said from the other side of the road but all of a sudden rifles had one up the spout and threats were being issued. I thought this is going a bit far, you know, threatening to shoot 'em. This was 1958, another decade and it would be different. The fellows got in their car and drove off. Next day the company commander sent for me. The top brass commended us for our control on the bridge, I got a pat on the back as corporal. The IRA had obviously been trying us out to see how far they could go.

On another occasion aerial photography had found a patch of disturbed ground. Had the IRA buried a cache of weapons? We had to go and investigate and having been in eighteen months I was now a veteran. The platoon lieutenant picked out eight men including me. 'Take the platoon and the Bren gun, Corporal!' It was almost like a section attack, all spread out and moving forward over this field in extended order and wondering what was going to happen. We finally got to the spot and found the farmer. Our officer asked him what was under the ground. He said one of his cows had died and he'd buried it: that was the end of it. That was the only time I felt I was going to be fired on.

I came out of the Army just before the end of November '58, from Hollywood Barracks in Belfast. I came out with a pal of mine, we'd gone in on the same day. I were sat on the bus to High Road Well and I saw this lad in front of me with a little bag and he looked nervous. I thought I've got a little bag and I bet I look nervous, I bet he's going to the same place as me and he was. Many years later I get tap on the shoulder, 'How's 23349419 going on?' I said, 'How'd you know my number?' He said that I was the one before him. We'd had that afternoon free as we waited for the night crossing, probably had a few drinks. I know we managed to get a cabin going back, a right luxury and some kip. We came back to Heysham, having gone over from Liverpool. Going over had been one of the worst moments I can remember having had five weeks after Cyprus. It was a rough sea, I was as sick as a dog, and now it was back to barrack room soldiering.

My lasting impression of Northern Ireland was of rain. Exercises, sports, leisure events, no matter what, it always seemed to be pouring down. Obviously we'd a few fine days but they seemed to be the exception. As it was real barrack room stuff the discipline was more pronounced, unlike Cyprus where you'd never see anyone from our own lot for weeks on end. You'd have to shave and make yourself clean and tidy but your clothes matched your circumstances. No shiny buttons or boots and the weather was a lot better than in Ireland. That said when we first got to the Troodos Mountains it was snowing and we wore cold/wet weather clothing.

I must tell you this as it was my only real bit of excitement, though I was in reality in no danger myself. When we first landed in Cyprus we were in the base camp on Nicosia racecourse before we went up to the mountains. We had odd jobs to do around camp. I remember one, building an officers' *basha*, a sort of Indian Army job, a roof and no sides to keep the sun off. On the notice board there were two courses available for which you'd put your name down. One was a driving course and the other was for stretcher bearers. My mate put down for the latter as he could drive. I couldn't so I opted for the driving course, it would very handy. Typical Army, of course, I got stretcher bearing and

Huddersfield war memorial, Greenhead Park. (Kirklees Archive)

he got driving. We went to Famagusta for a week and listened to a sergeant from the RAMC who gave demonstrations and talks on first aid and by dinner time you'd done. Very pleasant, Famagusta was a nice place with lovely beaches but then it was back to camp. Then it was, 'Quick, quick, get all your gear together, you're posted to 10 platoon, D company. In the Land Rover, you're going to join them up in the mountains.'

There were about four of us in the vehicle and as we were getting into the mountains we could hear this 'ratatatatat, bang, bang'. Bit of an exercise going on? The driver never said anything. We got there and it was more quick, quick, dump your kit in these two-man hike tents and help this captain load some avgas, aviation fuel, onto some donkeys – they used a lot of donkeys in Cyprus. They led the animals down to where they had the second in command of EOKA and two of his mates holed up in this cave. I had seen what preceded but on the way down in the pouring rain saw the body of one of our lads covered by his groundsheet. It transpired that there had been a reward out for these people and a local shepherd had succumbed to temptation and was showing us where these people were. However, he got cold feet on the approach and all he'd say was that it was somewhere over there, he'd go no nearer. Our company commander then had the lads strung out and they advanced slowly up this hill till they found something. Well, this corporal found a container full of weapons and called out. As he did so there was a shot from the cave and he was killed.

Geoff's memorabilia from the Dukes, including cap badge, brigade insignia and medal.

So, the decision was made that we were not going to lose any more men and these characters were anyway stuck in this cave and going nowhere. Keep pouring fire into the cave.

Eventually, three of these people made a bolt for it and our lads caught them. We had an interpreter who told one of them to go back inside and tell the last one to come out as he'd no chance of escape. Well, to give him his due he went back in and then shouted out, 'There's two of us now, come and get us'. That was enough and we stood over the cave entrance and dropped the avgas canisters into the mouth of the cave. Incoming fire blew them up but the fellow we sent in made another run for it. We caught him and the EOKA 2IC was killed and that was the end of that. I was, of course, perfectly safe where I was but that had been my first day out in the field and I was a bit concerned.

Of course, nothing like that happened. We used to do cordon and search, internal security duties when there was rioting, stuff like that. We'd also put out ambushes and before I'd got there a young 2nd Lieutenant thought he'd check that the lads were awake and alert. They were and he was shot dead. Your orders were simple: no one is to move up this path. Anyone who does will be shot on sight. He should have known better, only nineteen years old. We lost two other lads there.

Another night we heard this shot and thought hey up, we'll have to be alert. We were always in fours taking our positions covering a path and after a while we starting hearing voices. 'My girl's a Yorkshire girl', 'On Ilkley Moor bar t'at', it were some of our lads coming in and letting us know by singing Yorkshire songs. During these ambushes I used to lie there thinking if someone comes down here I'll let 'em get as far as that tree and let 'em have it. Never happened but you're left with the thought. I imagine I would have fired if it had come to it.

The Association

The Dukes are, of course, Huddersfield's local infantry regiment, always recruited strongly in this area. I got involved in the regimental history side through another chap, now dead. He asked me to come along and eventually you could expect to become chairman, I have been for the last seven years.

What it basically involves is finding speakers to come along to our regimental gatherings. It's not as easy as you might think it would be. We meet ten times a year and

I've got the first six covered and two for the last part of the year. These chaps come along and talk about all kinds of military and historical matters. Many of them are ex-soldiers and they're very good. We'd a chap from our regimental museum in Halifax come to talk about Waterloo and he came in full fig complete with a flintlock which health and safety now forbids him to fire.

The war memorial in Greenhead Park got to be in a terrible state, covered in graffiti. Now it's covered in anti-graffiti paint and is ring fenced. I go up usually on the 11 November and children are encouraged to go to the ceremony and lay flowers. I think this is a good thing as it makes you think not only about all these lads who died but also what they died for. The First World War still shocks, people did their duty and there was no media. My uncle died at the Somme, right at the end of it. As kids we used to play with his medals and dog tags, they were bloodstained and we used to boast about our uncle, as kids do.

Geoff, 2006.

In the Second World War the Dukes took terrible casualties in the Anzio Landing and then fought their way up the spine of Italy. There was a lot of bitterness over the American commander, Mark Clark. Why did the Allied Army not move inland straight away? To be fair, the Americans specifically asked the Dukes to lead the Allied Army's liberation parade through Rome and they did.

I recorded some tributes to English soldiers, there's one here. 'If they be well ordered and kept by the rules of good discipline, they fear not the face nor the force of the stoutest foe and have one singular virtue above any other nation for they are always willing to go on'. This one was from Charles Carrington who served as an officer in the First World War:

'It was not the comfort of a salary nor the fun of the officers' mess, nor the pony riding that made my time so satisfying, I was in love with my platoon. The whole of my thoughts and affections were for the forty Yorkshiremen with whom my life was so unexpectedly linked. They were a rough, tough lot but better or braver men in the world I have yet to find.'

Other local titles published by Tempus

Brighouse and District

CHRIS HELME

This fascinating collection of 200 archive photographs illustrates some of the historical developments which have shaped the town of Brighouse and its surrounding communities. The Industrial Revolution brought new prosperity to the area; this book describes the effects of industrialisation on the town and the people who helped to bring it about and explores the buildings, transport, shops and communities which have formed the heart of the area.

978 0 7524 3577 0

Buildings of Huddersfield

KEITH GIBSON AND ALBERT BOOTH

Huddersfield has a surprisingly rich architectural heritage. This book describes and illustrates around 200 of the best and most attractive structures to be seen in the town. It looks at the magnificent buildings of Victorian Huddersfield, at the much older manor and gentry houses, at churches, chapels and public buildings, at houses and at twentieth-century additions to the town, and will be a useful guide for those wishing to explore and learn more about Huddersfield's history through its buildings.

978 0 7524 3675 3

Honley: Then and Now

PETER BRAY AND HONLEY CIVIC SOCIETY

These 180 'then and now' photographs are but a small selection of the society's extensive record of the village over the years. Each pair encapsulates the changes that have occurred in the area over the last 100 years: the loss of buildings, industries and ways of life, the coming of the railways and the car. This remarkable book will stir the memories of old Honleyers and encourage newcomers to learn about their heritage and begin to cherish their village.

978 0 7524 4146 7

Huddersfield Pubs

DAVE GREEN

This is an illustrated, historical tour of the pubs and beer houses of Huddersfield and its environs by one of the town's best-known experts on the subject. The author has spent many years collecting old photographs, anecdotes and interesting information about the area's pubs and he draws on these resources and his considerable knowledge to compile this fascinating examination of the subject. His account also includes reference to the many local breweries as well as to the area's best known pub characters.

978 0 7524 4165 8